CW00329540

THE TOP 11 OF EVERYTHING RED

Manchester
United

IT'S NOT TRIVIA, IT'S MORE IMPORTANT THAN THAT

Written by Jim White and Andy Mitten

Text editors
Paul Simpson, Helen Rodiss,
Michaela Bushell,
Mark Ellingham

Production
Ian Cranna, Tim Oldham,
Tim Harrison

Cover and book design
Sharon O'Connor

Cover image
Cocoon/Digital Vision

Thanks to
Iain McCartney, Sam Pilger,
Ian McLeish, Simon Kanter,
Andrew Lockett

Printed in Spain
by Graphy Cems

This edition published
July 2005 was prepared by
Haymarket Network for
Rough Guides Ltd,
80 Strand, London, WC2R ORL

Distributed by the
Penguin Group
Penguin Books Ltd,
27 Wrights Lane,
London W8 5TZ

A catalogue record for this
book is available from the
British Library

ISBN 1-84353-559-9

Contents

ABSOLUTE BEST RED MOMENTS

Sometimes football really is magic...

1. Sir Matt Busby sings *What A Wonderful World* while standing on a table in the Russell Hotel, London

On the night of 29 May 1968 – ten years after the Munich air disaster – Busby's cherished United have become the first English club to win the European Cup. The Boss takes his turn for a karaoke moment at the celebratory party, and there's not a dry eye in the house. When he finishes his rendition of Louis Armstrong's *What A Wonderful World*, Busby is asked whether he was thinking of the fallen Munich team as he sang. Almost choked with the emotional significance of the evening, he replies: "Deep down the sorrow is there all the time. It becomes part of you." Bobby Charlton, now captain, prefers a more literal response. When asked: "How did it feel to lift the trophy ten years after walking from the Munich wreckage?" Charlton replies: "It felt bloody heavy."

2. George Best decides he's seen enough and heads for the bar...

It's 26 May 1999, and Bestie is in the Camp Nou, Barcelona, watching United – who have already secured the domestic Double – trailing Bayern Munich 1-0 in the final of the Champions League. There are barely two minutes left and, frankly, the United legend is a little thirsty. Besides, he cannot bear to hang around and watch the inevitable German celebration. But he hasn't reckoned on the indomitable spirit and resolve of Alex Ferguson's team, on Teddy Sheringham's poaching skills and Ole Gunnar Solskjaer's extendable toe. By the time he reaches the bar, Manchester United have won 2-1, to become the one and only English club to win the Treble.

3. John Henry Davies meets Harry Stafford's dog

April, 1902. Harry Stafford, Newton Heath's full-back and captain, is out collecting money for his club, which is heading for bankruptcy. His dog, Major, a collecting box round his neck, goes walkies and ends up in a pub owned by Davies, boss of

Manchester Breweries. Davies's daughter takes a shine to Major, and together they track down Stafford, who agrees to sell them the dog, provided Davies invests in Newton Heath. Davies is intrigued, says he'll see what he can do and within a year is chairman of a new club called Manchester United. He underwrites a new stadium to be built at Old Trafford in 1910. So important does he become to the club that his death, in 1927, heralds the most desperate period in United's history.

4. Alex Ferguson fails to heed Alan Hansen's warning

Alex Ferguson's first Double with United in 1994 is achieved with a quick, wily, tough team of battle-hardened pros. Within 18 months he has dismantled it, replacing many old favourites with callow specimens from his youth operation. He is told by Alan Hansen on *Match Of The Day* that he'd better buy some new players quick, because "you'll win nothing with kids". Fergie doesn't listen and his hungry, young, homespun prodigies win the Double in 1996. That the Cup final victory is over Hansen's old club Liverpool makes the achievement all the sweeter.

5. Louis Rocca writes to Matt Busby

Rocca, United's assistant manager and chief scout, has been trying to trace Busby for a month as World War 2 comes to a close, believing him to be the man to revive the war-shattered football club as soon as the hostilities are over. Worried about sending correspondence to Liverpool – Busby's previous employers – Rocca writes, on 15 December 1944, a coded, conspiratorial letter to the Busby family home in which he talks of "having a great job for you". He implores Busby to get in touch with him at Old Trafford. Eventually – they didn't have email in 1944 – Busby obliges, and, as soon as he is demobbed at the war's conclusion, he takes up the position of Manchester United manager. He is actively involved at the club for over 30 years.

6. The end of the 26-year wait

A generation of Reds grew up understanding that Liverpool won the league and United didn't. By the early 1990s, however, fortunes were shifting, although United still let the 1992 title slip away – and effectively at Anfield, too. That day, Liverpool fans held up a mocking banner saying: "Form is temporary, class is permanent." United's class arrives the following season. "Eric Cantona brings a priceless presence and style to the team," declared his manager. With Cantona as the catalyst, the 26-year wait for the league title finally comes to an end on 2 May 1993 when Oldham beat second-placed Aston Villa. The following night, Blackburn Rovers visit Old Trafford, the trophy is presented and the crowd (including Sir Matt) are unashamedly dewy-eyed in celebration. Here's how Cantona recalls the celebrations: "We brandished the cup before Sir Matt Busby, the man whose most beautiful children had perished in that air catastrophe. We did a lap of honour to cheers from all around the ground. When I compare this spectacle to all the shows in the world, this isn't far from being the most perfect because, just as in certain theatres, the audience is almost part of the play. I went back into the dressing rooms. The champagne could flow all night. My shower was long and enjoyable. I didn't go to the celebrations which were given in our honour. I wanted to get home to Leeds to be with my young son."

7. Blackpool's rock goes limp

It's the 1948 FA Cup final at Wembley and Blackpool appear to be cruising to victory. Still ahead against Manchester United in the 70th minute, Stan Mortensen and the boys assume they are destined for glory. But Matt Busby's lads first bring the score level at 2-2, then blitz the Seasiders to complete a memorable 4-2 win. It's a particularly significant victory. It's Busby's first trophy in only his third season at United and marks the first time since World War 1 that the Reds are the pre-eminent club in Manchester.

8. Liverpool find an FA Cup-shaped space in their trophy cabinet

On the afternoon of 21 May 1977, with the league championship in the bag and the European Cup final to follow, a rampant Liverpool believe victory over Manchester United in the FA Cup final is as good as a formality – the easiest part of an unprecedented Treble. They are not alone in thinking this. "We were not too confident," admits Stuart Pearson, United's first goalscorer that day. "We knew we'd give Liverpool a game but they were so good that you could never say: 'Right, we're going to beat these.'" But beat them Pearson and the Reds do, a thrilling 2-1 victory, thus ensuring the elusive grail of the first Treble will remain intact for a future generation of United players.

9. United fans risk pneumonia in a Rotterdam downpour

It is 15 May 1991, the five-year ban on English clubs following the Heysel tragedy has been relaxed, and United have reached the Cup Winners' Cup final. Their opponents are Barcelona. As the rain falls ceaselessly on Red fans in the open sections of the ground, the noise is indomitable. All the Madchester anthems of the time are given a communal run through, before the fans decide *Always Look On The Bright Side Of Life* best sums up their soggy predicament. And what a bright side it is: Mark Hughes scores twice to give Alex Ferguson his first taste of European glory with United. By the end of the decade he is back for more.

10. Highbury rises as one to salute the Busby Babes

The date: 1 February 1958. The time: 4.45pm. The home side has just lost 4-5 to United, but the Arsenal fans know they have witnessed something special. United's

11. v ARSENAL 2005

Carroll

G. Neville   Heinze
Silvestre (sent off)   Ferdinand

Scholes   Keane   Fletcher
Ronaldo   Giggs

Rooney

1 February 2005
Premiership,
Highbury.
Arsenal 2 (Vieira,
Bergkamp), Manchester
United 4 (Ronaldo 2,
Rooney, O'Shea).
Sir Alex thought this was
the best-ever game since
the Premiership began.
He may well be right.

young team, known now as the Busby Babes, have been unstoppable. Three up at half-time, the Babes produce a performance that proves to a sceptical London press that they are the greatest English club side since Herbert Chapman's Arsenal in the 1930s. Everyone there to see the game is convinced that a third consecutive championship lies ahead for the visitors. But first, they have a trip to Belgrade.

11. Matt Busby decides to ignore the blazers

In 1955, insular as ever, the xenophobic blazers of the Football League decide in their wisdom that English teams will not demean themselves by taking part in the new-fangled continental invention known as the European Cup. Chelsea, First Division champions (for the last time in 50 years), are told not to accept an invitation to participate. A year later, the new English champions come over all hard of hearing, enter the competition despite official instruction, and on 26 September 1956, Manchester United play the first-ever competitive game on English soil against a European side. That they win 10-0 against Anderlecht is only a footnote. More importantly, the love affair with Europe has begun.

THAT THEY WIN 10-0
AGAINST ANDERLECHT
IS ONLY A FOOTNOTE.
THE LOVE AFFAIR WITH
EUROPE HAS BEGUN

THE ATTENDANCE TODAY... [1]

The 11 biggest Reds crowds, excluding Cup finals. Interestingly, all home figures were recorded while United were playing at Maine Road

1. **135,000** Real Madrid (a), April 1957
2. **125,000** Real Madrid (a), May 1968
3. **114,432** Barcelona (a), November 1994
4. **105,000** Gornik Zabrze (a), March 1968
5. **82,771** Bradford Park Avenue (h), January 1949
6. **81,962** Arsenal (h), January 1948
7. **81,565** Yeovil Town (h), February 1949
8. **80,000** AC Milan (a), May 1958
   AC Milan (a), April 1969
10. **75,598** Borussia Dortmund (h), October 1956
11. **75,000** Benfica (a), March 1966
   Manchester City (a), January 1955

THE ATTENDANCE TODAY... [2]

You must have come in a taxi...the 11 lowest United crowds since 1945

1. **4,670** Bradford City (a), November 1960
2. **5,400** Athinaikos (a), September 1991
3. **6,527** Djurgården (a), September 1964
4. **6,730** Panathinaikos (a), November 2003
5. **6,841** Halifax Town (a), September 1990
6. **8,000** FC Lodz (a), August 1998
7. **8,168** Verona (a), May 1973
8. **8,456** Stoke City (h), February 1947
9. **8,966** Oxford United (a), May 1988
10. **9,000** Kispest Honved (a), September 1993
11. **9,033** Exeter City (a), January 2005

BANNERS

The wit and wisdom of the Stretford End

1. Joe Royle's fat head
Reds in Valencia in 2000 offer their appreciation of the incredibly large cranium of the then-City boss.

2. Atkinson's long leather
Fair play to Liverpool fans for picking up on the sartorial faux pas of United's flashiest manager. But what did they expect from a fellow Scouser?

3. We all know that Manchester is Red
Just how do United fans get the flag into City's Kippax Stand in 2002? Better still, how do they get City fans to pass it above their heads?

4. 17 years
The original banner which pointed out the number of years since City won a trophy is unveiled in Budapest in 1993. A version – updated annually – now adorns the Stretford End.

> ONE CHAPTER IN THE BEST SOCCER ANNUAL WAS TITLED 'FOOTBALLERS HAVE BRAINS'

5. MUFC the religion
Another current Stretford End reworking.

6. MUFC – We're too sexy for Milan
Aloft at the San Siro, 1999.

7. 6 Feb 1958 – the flowers of Manchester
Found its rightful home on the Stretford End.

8. Republic of Mancunia – Red Army
Another current Stretford End number.

9. Big lily
That's the name of the giant red, white and black flag owned by Carrickfergus Red Keith.

10. Buchan defender of the faith
A 1997 Wembley encouragement.

11. Play up United – give it Joe
One of the oldest known – a banner for 1919-33 star Joe Spence.

BEST BEST BOOKS

Where did it all go wrong, George? We'll take these tomes chronologically. (For more United books see Lit Crit)

1. George Best Soccer Annual 1968–72
An early bit of merchandising, Best's contributions includes chapters such as 'Footballers Have Brains' and 'Busy, Busy Time.' Sample prose:"Each morning I am called at home about nine, have a quick breakfast, normally cooked as I'm a great one for food, and then out comes the current car, a great yellow Lotus Europa at the time of writing, then off to training. And under Wilf McGuinness that's no cake walk."

2. George Best: Anatomy Of A Football Star David Meek, 1970
The *Manchester Evening News'* man-on-the-spot gives us a view of Best before the fall. The book is tinged with unintended irony:"Whatever the future holds, George Best is prepared for it."

3. George Best, Fall Of A Superstar John Roberts and Derek Hodgson, 1973
And you can bet when they write it, the authors never thought he'd still be falling 32 years on.

4. Best: An Intimate Biography Michael Parkinson, 1974
The chat-show meister is a good friend to Bestie, and provides sanctuary from the madness in the years on the run. But that does not prevent him offering up this warts-and-all account of football's first broken hero.

11. v BARCELONA 1991

Sealey

Blackmore — Irwin
Pallister — Bruce

Phelan — Robson — Ince — Sharpe

Hughes — McClair

15 May 1991
Cup Winners' Cup final,
Rotterdam.
Manchester United 2
(Hughes 2) Barcelona 1
(Koeman).
The first European trophy
won by an English club
since the Heysel ban
was lifted.

5. Where Do I Go From Here? An Autobiography George Best with Geoffrey Wright, 1981
In which our hero delivers an array of defensive barbs about "my so-called critics" and invocations that he will come back and show the world. Sadly, at the time actions speak louder than words.

6. The Good, The Bad And The Bubbly George Best with Ross Benson, 1991
A largely tawdry collection of yarns, although it did introduce the one about Bestie in the hotel room with Miss World in her negligée, the winnings from the casino all over the bed and the little Irish hotel porter who, even as he eases the cork from the champagne bottle, asks where it all went wrong.

7. The Best Of Times: My Favourite Soccer Stories George Best with Les Scott, 1995
Bestie teams up with the *Stoke Sentinel*'s top man for another rehash of all those yarns; the hotel porter once more takes centre stage.

8. Bestie: Portrait Of A Legend Joe Lovejoy, 1998
Easily the most persuasive portrait, penned with full co-operation from the man

11. v BAYERN MUNICH 1999

Schmeichel

G. Neville   Irwin

Stam   Johnsen

Giggs   Beckham   Butt   Blomqvist

Cole   Yorke

26 May 1999
Champions League final,
Barcelona.
Manchester United 2
(Sheringham, Solskjaer)
Bayern 1 (Basler).
The greatest night in United
history as the Treble is secured.
You may remember that
Sheringham came on for
Blomqvist and Solskjaer
replaced Cole.

himself by the *Sunday Times* football correspondent (who looks eerily like Best).
The book opens with an eye-wateringly painful account of a drunken Best brawling
in a snooker hall during a public appearance.

9. Blessed: The Autobiography George Best with Roy Collins, 2001
Bestie's fourth autobiography (and the 33rd book about him) hits the top of the
bestsellers' list, even though it told us little that Lovejoy hadn't. Oh, and would you
believe it, the hotel porter gets the come on down.

10. George And Me: My Autobiography Angie Best with Nicola Pittam, 2001
Wonder how many copies of her life story Angie MacDonald James would have
shifted had she not become Mrs Best?

11. Scoring At Half Time George Best, 2003
Red-top collection of tales of romps and bonks gathered from "Bestie's showbiz and
sporting pals". His own contribution includes, you've guessed it, that little Irish hotel
porter. The guy should charge commission. That's if he ever existed.

BEST BEST FLAMES

Miss World and the rest. Here's a selective run-down from El Beatle's heyday in the 1960s to present times

1. Georgie Ellis
The model and daughter of Ruth, the last woman ever to be hanged in Britain, Georgie is Best's first high-profile girlfriend. The relationship ends in 1967 after she gets pregnant and has an abortion.

2. Susan George
The 1970s screen siren makes her movie debut in 1965 in *Cup Fever*, a movie which features several United players including Best. He waits until 1969 to move in on her, but she ditches him after a six-week fling.

3. Sinead Cusack
Later to become a renowned Shakespearean actress and Mrs Jeremy Irons, Sinead meets Best on the set of a Dublin chat show in 1970. He flees to her place the first time he walks out on United, and is tracked down by the press pack to her flat in Islington the night before a big game against Chelsea.

4. Carolyn Moore
Miss Great Britain 1971 and a Miss World entrant, Carolyn Moore provides Bestie with his first taste of the beauty pageant that will become his favoured courting territory for the next couple of decades. He drops her in 1971 after she has a session with another footballer.

5. Marjorie Wallace
The American model is Bestie's first Miss World winner, in 1974. She was the one in the hotel room with the Irish porter (see Best Best Books).

6 Lynsey de Paul
The pint-sized singer-songwriter gives Bestie the runaround in 1975. Her last hit, incidentally, is *Rock Bottom*, an all-too prescient summary of George Best's subsequent career.

7. Angie MacDonald James
Angie becomes the first Mrs Best in 1978, and the statuesque blonde ex-model lives with Best in America throughout his flirtation with the Los Angeles Aztecs. Their son Callum is born in Los Angeles in 1981 before Best leaves Angie for – would you believe it – Miss World.

v BENFICA 1968

Stepney

Brennan · Dunne

Stiles · Foulkes · Crerand

Aston · Charlton · Sadler · Kidd · Best

29 May 1968
European Cup final,
Wembley.
Manchester United 4
(Charlton 2, Best, Kidd)
Benfica 1 (Torres).
Sir Matt's finest hour,
ten years after his
darkest moment.

8. Mary Stavin

The Swedish Miss World takes on George in the aftermath of the breakdown of his marriage. The couple launch a fitness video in 1983, though, for some reason, George's daily health regime at the time (a bottle of vodka washed down by a couple of bottles of white wine) doesn't feature.

9. Eva Haraldsted

Another tall, blonde Scandinavian Miss World entrant who catches Bestie's eye in the late 1980s. Yes, there is a pattern.

10. Mary Shatila

Shatila is an unusual Best squeeze: she is a brunette. The pair started dating after our hero spots her at a nightclub he owned at the time – called, inevitably, Blondes. She is his personal manager for several years, before he turns her over in favour of…

11. Alex Pursey

They meet on a plane (she is, naturally, the hostess) and, despite a 20-year age gap, Alex becomes the second Mrs Best in 1995. She is by his side through a liver transplant, his attempts to turn teetotal and, most challenging of all, a brief escape from the celebrity lifestyle to a fishing village in Northern Ireland. They divorce in 2004 after he falls, spectacularly, off the wagon. She is last seen trying to avoid Lord Brockett's wandering hands on *I'm A Celebrity Get Me Out Of Here!*

BEST NEW BESTS

It's a bit of a curse...

1. John Aston
Dark-haired, quick and played for United. And that was about all he had in common with his European Cup-winning colleague.

2. Willie Morgan
Loathed the NGB moniker and to this day will tell anyone who makes it that he had a fan club up and running long before Best. The pair never got on after Morgan arrived from Burnley, though Morgan did once help Best out by substituting for the great man on a date with Germaine Greer. But that's another story.

3. Trevor Anderson
Young, Irish and dark-browed: enough for the label to be attached to a player with marginally less talent than Best possessed in his big toe. Signed from Portadown by Frank O'Farrell, but Tommy Docherty quickly sold him on to Swindon Town.

4. Sammy McIlroy
Another young Ulsterman in United colours. But he was never going to be the NGB. He was bald by the time he was 35, for a start.

5. Norman Whiteside
There may have been no physical similarities, but both shared a Celtic appetite for self-destruction. Both were finished at United way ahead of time.

6. Jesper Olsen
Buck-toothed Dane whose only similarity to Best was that they both played on the wing. Best was quicker, though. When he was 50.

7. Ryan Giggs
The most persuasive NGB was covered with embarrassment when, on a video the pair did to mark the young Welsh winger's arrival in the first team, Bestie proclaimed he would like to have been known as the First Ryan Giggs. A subsequent 14-year

11. v BLACKPOOL 1948

Crompton

Carey   Aston

Chilton   Anderson

Cockburn

Mitten   Morris   Delaney

Rowley   Pearson

24 April 1948
FA Cup final,
Wembley.
Manchester United 4 (Rowley 2,
Pearson, Anderson)
Blackpool 2 (Mortensen,
Shimwell). Busby's first trophy;
12 more were to follow.

career at the top suggests Giggs had nothing to be embarrassed about; Bestie must envy staying power like that.

8. Calum Best
His dad persuaded Fergie to give the lad a trial. Afterwards the two men agreed the youngster was probably better cut out for a career in modelling.

9. David Beckham
His commercial appeal was initially compared to Best, the first pop-star footballer. But Beckham has long since out-stripped him financially.

10. Cristiano Ronaldo
A lazy comparison, as Bestie could never have done all those step-overs. At least not after a night at Slack Alice's.

11. Wayne Rooney
Predicted in the press to be a tragedy waiting to happen, the pugilistic Scouser has yet to show evidence of a Best-style derailment. There is another reason why it is a fatuous comparison: never in his 40-year career has Bestie needed to pay for it.

BOSSES

No prizes for guessing the top two...

1. Sir Alex Ferguson 1986–present
Who's arguing? He's won the Champions League once, the league title eight times, the FA Cup five times, the Cup Winners' Cup once and the League Cup once.

2. Sir Matt Busby 1945–69, 1970–71
Single-handedly rebuilt the club after the war. Won the European Cup once, the league title five times and the FA Cup twice.

3. J. Ernest Magnall 1903–12
The first United manager. Won the title twice and the FA Cup once.

4. Ron Atkinson 1981–86
Sun-bed fanatic turned disgraced telly pundit. Runner-up in the league, won the FA Cup twice, runner-up in the League Cup.

5. Tommy Docherty 1972–77
Won the FA Cup once, runner-up once, won the Second Division title.

6. Dave Sexton 1977–81
Runner-up in the league once and the FA Cup once. Dull.

7. Scott Duncan 1932–37
Yo-yo manager. Won the Second Division title, relegated the next year, runner-up in the Second Division the year after that.

8. John Chapman 1921–26
Promoted as Second Division runner-up but resigned after presiding over the club's record defeat: 0–7 away at Blackburn Rovers on 10 April 1926.

9. Herbert Bramlett 1927–31
In charge during the record sequence without a league win: 16 games in 1930.

10. Frank O'Farrell 1971–72
Hopeless.

11. Wilf McGuinness 1969–70
Brief, disastrous successor to Busby.

CAPTAINS OF TROPHY-WINNING TEAMS

Chronological again – the first eight won the league title, the other three won other reasonably significant baubles...

1. **Charlie Roberts** 1908, 1911
2. **Johnny Carey** 1952
3. **Roger Byrne** 1956, 1957
4. **Denis Law** 1965
5. **Bobby Charlton** 1967
6. **Steve Bruce** 1993, 1994, 1996
7. **Eric Cantona** 1997
8. **Roy Keane** 1999, 2000, 2001, 2003
9. **Noel Cantwell** FA Cup 1963
10. **Bryan Robson** FA Cup 1983
11. **Peter Schmeichel** European Cup 1999

CLEOPATRA'S NOSE MOMENTS

Historians suggest that if Cleopatra's nose had not been quite so perfectly formed, then Marc Antony would never have taken such a shine to her and the history of the ancient world would have been entirely changed. Here are 11 incidents – seemingly minor at the time – that altered irreparably the course of Red history

1. Fergie picks Mark Robins for the FA Cup third-round tie against Nottingham Forest January 1990

The manager's tenure at Old Trafford is teetering on the edge and virtually every pundit predicts that defeat against Cloughie's boys will signal his departure. Driven on by rampant support, United's hitherto dodgy collection of new recruits matches a more cultured Forest side stride for stride. Then the young lad from Ashton stoops to head in Mark Hughes's pass. Ironically it was Robins who would fail to make the grade with United but, over the past decade, hardly a day has gone by without him being reminded of the significance of that goal.

2. Fergie scribbles a name on a piece of paper as Martin Edwards talks on the phone to the Leeds United chairman September 1992
Leeds want to buy Denis Irwin. United are having none of it but Fergie, mischievously, writes a note asking his chairman to inquire if a certain Eric Cantona is available for transfer. Just imagine if he had written down the words 'Lee' and 'Chapman' instead.

3. Tommy Docherty is introduced to Mary Brown, the wife of the club's physio Laurie Brown spring 1976
The Doc is beginning to gain control of a club badly adrift following Sir Matt Busby's retirement five years earlier. With an FA Cup win under his belt, the Doc would have been unassailable – had he only kept his nose clean. But love has a habit of getting in the way, and his affair with Mrs Brown provides his enemies within the Old Trafford hierarchy with the ammunition they need to bring him down. Not to mention providing rival fans with their favourite chant for years to come: "Who's up Mary Brown?"

4. Louis Rocca rejects Manchester Central April 1902
Feeling they need a name which reflects the club's growth, the directors are discussing alternatives to Newton Heath FC. Rocca declares he doesn't much fancy the favourite, Manchester Central. He reckons it sounds more like the name of a railway station (which it was) than a football club. He asks for other suggestions and someone, listed only as 'a voice', shouts "Manchester United".

IF IT HADN'T BEEN FOR POSH SPICE. UNITED MAY NEVER HAVE BOUGHT RONALDO

5. Michael Knighton is turned down for a bank loan August 1989
Knighton appears on the pitch before the first game of the season, playing keepy-uppy and blasting the ball into the Stretford End net. But this moustached, fly-by-night property developer from the Isle of Man does not quite have the wherewithal to buy United that he claims to have. One by one, his backers drop out and his audacious bid unravels. And all he needs is £10m, roughly an 80th of what the club is worth a decade later. He turns his attention instead to Carlisle United, and sets about making them the force they are today.

11. v CHELSEA 1994

Schmeichel

Parker Pallister Bruce Irwin

Kanchelskis Keane Ince Giggs

Hughes Cantona

14 May 1994
FA Cup final,
Wembley.
Manchester United 4 (Cantona
2, McClair, Hughes) Chelsea 0.
Alex Ferguson does what even
Sir Matt could not achieve:
he wins his first Double, with
a team many consider his
strongest-ever United line-up.

6. Patrick Vieira gives the ball to Ryan Giggs on the halfway line at Villa Park April 1999

You know what happens next, but it's always worth the repetition: see p45.

7. Victoria Adams is invited to Old Trafford as a guest of Martin Edwards March 1996

The Spice Girl gives David Beckham her phone number and Becks calls up. As the relationship blossoms and the pair become so famous they are described as an alternative royal family. Beckham's change in lifestyle so alarms his manager that he is eventually sold off to Real Madrid. United pocket the rather pitiful sum of £25m for a player who generates that much in merchandise alone. On the football front, however, the jury is still out. Had Beckham stayed, United would not have bought Cristiano Ronaldo – for half DB's fee.

8. Sir Alex Ferguson looks a gift horse in the eye August 2001

The horse is called Rock of Gibraltar and Sir Alex's racing pal, John Magnier – who Fergie encourages to buy into United – gives the Boss a half share. The nag becomes racing legend, winning seven class-one races on the bounce in 2002, and stacking up £1,269,800 in prize money. But the real cash in racing is in stud fees. When the Rock is sent off to pleasure the mares of the world in 2003, it is reckoned he could generate a cool £200m. Sir Alex assumes he is due half, Magnier thinks otherwise, and the lawyers are called in. Eventually the case is settled out of court, but the damage is done: by now Magnier has bought big time into United and the public airing of dirty laundry between leading shareholder and leading employee is not good news. In May 2005, Magnier and partner JP McManus make a tidy profit by selling their 28.7% holding to the Florida-based leprechaun Malcolm Glazer. Whether the sale is motivated by profit, revenge or both, the ever-reticent Magnier isn't saying.

9. Manchester United snare Ryan Wilson (nee Giggs) from City 1988
The Blues' talented young side, which finished above United in 1991, lose out on the most exciting player of his generation. As City slip and slide throughout the rest of the 1990s, United, with Giggs, become the   pre-eminent team in England.

10. Paul Scholes has a legitimate goal disallowed in the Champions League game against Porto at Old Trafford February 2004
If it had counted, United would have progressed to the quarter-final. Porto would not have won the trophy, their manager José Mourinho would not have done his over-excited jig down the touchline and would not now be in charge of Chelsea.

11. Captain James Thain decides to risk a third attempt to take off from Munich airport 6 February 1958
If only he had waited for the next day.

COCK-UP AT THE FONT

11 unusual player names

1. **Norbert Stiles** 1960-71
2. **Horace Blew** 1905-06
3. **Sam Blott** 1909-13
4. **Dick Pegg** 1902-04
5. **Clayton Blackmore** 1983-94
6. **Leslie Lievesley** 1931-32
7. **Fred Erantz** 1892-1902
8. **Gilbert Godsmark** 1899-1900
9. **Walter Winterbottom** 1936-38
10. **Lancelot Holliday Richardson** 1925-29
11. **Ole Gunnar Solskjaer** 1996-

COCKNEY REDS

You're 'aving a larf: a chirpy line-up of Red-breasted sparrers managed, presumably, by London-born Dave Sexton

1. Les Sealey
Born in Walthamstow. Madder than a bucket of snakes, a heroic stand-in keeper who roared through life on the edge, before his all-too-early death in 2001.

2. Paul Parker
Born in West Ham. Nimble, speedy little full-back who found himself eased out by the emergence of decidedly non-Cockney Gary Neville.

3. Tommy Gipps
Born in Walthamstow. A regular defender in the final season before World War 1. Gipps was called up to the Front and survived, but never played for the Reds again.

4. Ray Wilkins
Born in Hillingdon. Dubbed The Crab by Ron Atkinson for passing sideways so much, but managed to kick it forward at least once, scoring a belter in the 1983 FA Cup final.

5. David Sadler
Born in Yalding. An all-rounder in the great Busby side of the 1960s, Sadler played emergency centre-forward in the European Cup final, in for the injured Denis Law.

6. Paul Ince
Born in Ilford. The Guvnor had five seasons as a Red before leaving for Italy.

7. David Beckham
Born in Leytonstone. Remember this geezer – the one with the hair? Oddly, Becks never honoured his birthplace in one of his children's names: Leytonstone is surely no worse than Brooklyn, Romeo or Cruz.

8. Danny Wallace
Born in Greenwich. Ron Atkinson acquired Danny from Southampton, where he was one of three brothers to play for the club (twins Rod and Raymond were the others).

IF PAUL SCHOLES GOAL AGAINST PORTO HAD COUNTED, MOURINHO WOULD NOT NOW BE MANAGING CHELSEA

9. Teddy Sheringham
Born in Highams Park. A Hammers fan as a kid but blooded at Millwall, Teddy arrived from Spurs and will be forever enshrined in Red folklore, having won the lot.

10. Laurie Cunningham
Born in Archway. This jet-heeled winger made his name with Real Madrid long before he arrived for a brief five-match loan period at the end of the 1983 season. Sadly, he died six years later in a car crash in Spain.

11. Gordon Hill
Born in Sunbury-on-Thames. A birthday on April Fool's Day just about summed up the man who liked to call himself Merlin.

COMMERCIAL BREAKS

United players star in adverts across the globe...

1. George Best and Cookstown Sausages
Bestie cements his position as the first football pop star with an ad in 1968 for Cookstown Sausages, only available in Northern Ireland. "Delicious," he insists.

2. Bobby Charlton and Shredded Wheat
It takes World Cup-winner Bobby Charlton some time to get in on the advert lark but he finally makes his debut, alongside brother Jack, in a 1996 commercial for Shredded Wheat.

3. Tommy Docherty and Gillette
Just before the 1976 Cup final, Tommy Docherty, Steve Coppell and Gordon Hill do a telly ad for Gillette with the catchphrase "Give your beard the old one-two". Since there are three of them, the tag-line's relevance is a little misty.

4. Joe Jordan and Heineken
Heineken's claim that it reaches the parts other beer cannot reach takes an unlikely turn when a poster suggesting the beer has restored a full set of gnashers to the notoriously tooth-free Joe Jordan appears ahead of the 1978 World Cup.

5. Ryan Giggs eats Quorn
A youthful Ryan Giggs emerges from Fergie's total media exclusion zone in 1994 with an endorsement for Quorn, a veggie-friendly meat substitute. As an actor he

never totally convinces, but then Robert De Niro would have problems looking sincere promoting that product.

6. Le Dieu and Nike

Eric Cantona becomes the face of Nike in 1994, and during Euro 96 his face appears on posters which read: "1966 was a great year for English football: Eric was born". United fans love it.

7. Big Peter and Reebok

In an ad for Reebok, Peter Schmeichel tells the world that without a decent pair of football boots he might have ended up as a pig farmer back home in rural Denmark. Odd, really, as you would think goalkeepers rely more on their gloves.

8. Becks and Police

For the 2002 World Cup, much of Tokyo's bus fleet is redecorated with an image of David Beckham looking cool in Police sunglasses. In the summer of 2003, he and the wife earn £1m for a day's work promoting a Japanese supermarket chain. Together with endorsements for Pepsi, Adidas and Gillette, it means he trousers more than £12m in off-the-field activity in one year. Nice work if you can get it.

9. Becks, the Nevilles and Vodafone

Soon after their pal departs for the Bernabeu, the Neville brothers film a commercial for Vodafone in which Becks sends pictures to their mobiles of Spanish sky and big villas, which they receive while sitting in a tent in rainy old Blighty. Their manager is less than pleased, and gives them an almighty bollocking for looking like a pair of love-lorn prats.

10. Keane eats Kit Kat

In an advert for Kit Kat which asks us to challenge our expectations, Roy Keane is found in the United dressing room doing embroidery. Rumours that he is stitching up Patrick Vieira are wide of the mark.

11. Rooney calls Vodafone

Wayne Rooney appears in Vodafone commercials. Though he scrubs up reasonably well, everyone agrees he is probably not destined to become the next David Beckham.

DEFEATS IN EUROPE

Let's be honest – it's the European competition we all care about. And these are the matches that halted our progress

1. Fenerbahce
The first team to win a European game at Old Trafford wasn't AC Milan, Barça or Real Madrid, but Fenerbahce of Istanbul, 1-0 winners in October 1996.

2. Sporting Lisbon
Blitzed United 5–0 away in the 1963/64 Cup Winners' Cup. Which meant that the 4-1 home victory and Denis Law's hat-trick counted for little.

3. Tottenham Hotspur
Spurs beat United 2-0 in the 1964 Cup Winners' Cup. But United went on to win the home leg 4-1.

4. Barcelona
Barça put four past United without reply in a key Champions League game in 1994. Never repeat the words Stoichkov and Romario to Steve Bruce or Gary Pallister.

5. Maccabi Haifa
The Israeli champions beat a youthful United side 3-0 in 2002. The game was played in Nicosia, Cyprus, due to the security situation in Israel.

> ATLETICO BILBAO HANDED UNITED THEIR FIRST DEFEAT IN EUROPE IN 1957

6. Atletico Bilbao
The Basques beat United 5-3 in a snowy fixture in 1957. It was United's first defeat in Europe, but they overturned the result back at Old Trafford, winning 3-0 in the second leg.

7. Milan
The Rossoneri said later they had expected this Champions League knock-out tie to be a tougher contest. And so did we. Didn't help that a Chelsea reject scored both Milan goals.

8. Juventus
United lost three of the six Champions League group games in the 1996/97 season, but still qualified behind Juventus, who had edged United 1-0 home and away.

9. Borussia Dortmund
The Germans managed the same scorelines in the semi-final of that year's Champions League competition.

10. Bayern Munich
Fired up by their defeat in the 1999 European Cup final, Bayern Munich beat United home and away the next time the clubs met in 2001.

11. Gornik Zabrze
United's only defeat on the successful 1968 European Cup-winning campaign was against Gornik Zabrze in Poland. Actually, United didn't win a single away game en route to the Wembley final, drawing the other three.

DEPARTURES

"There's only one way from here, son, and that's down." Here are 11 record-breaking departures from United

1. **Alan Gowling** £60,000 to Huddersfield Town, June 1972
2. **Ted McDougall** £170,000 to West Ham, March 1973
3. **Gordon Hill** £275,000 to Derby Country, April 1978
4. **Brian Greenhoff** £350,000 to Leeds United, August 1979
5. **Andy Ritchie** £500,000 to Brighton, October 1980
6. **Ray Wilkins** £1.4m to Milan, June 1984
7. **Mark Hughes** £1.8m to FC Barcelona, August 1986
8. **Dion Dublin** £1.95m to Coventry City, September 1994
9. **Paul Ince** £6m to Internazionale, June 1995
10. **Jaap Stam** £16.5m to Lazio, September 2001
11. **David Beckham** £25m to Real Madrid, July 2003

11. v DARWEN 1898

Barrett
Stafford
F. Errentz
Draycott
Pepper
Cartwright
Bryant
Collinson
Boyd
Cassidy
Gillespie

24 December 1898
United 9 (Bryant 3, Cassidy 3, Gillespie 2 and an own goal)
Darwen 0
This is the team published in the first matchday programme for Newton Heath FC. The programme was a joint issue: it also covered Manchester City, Salford and Broughton Rangers rugby clubs. In those days, players' first names were never used.

DUG-OUT REDS

They learned it all at the Cliff and now they're coaches themselves

1. Steve Bruce
Birmingham's man, at least until a better offer comes along.

2. Bryan Robson
Miracle worker at the Hawthorns.

3. Mark Hughes
Putting some steel back into Blackburn Rovers.

4. Steve Coppell
Clever winger, now runs Reading.

5. Barry Fry
Fringe Busby Babe, recently moved from the dugout to the boardroom at Peterborough United, the original Posh.

6. Sammy McIlroy
Skipped from Northern Ireland to Macclesfield, to Stockport County, to MUTV in four short steps.

7. Brian McClair
Fergie's favourite remains in touch with the Boss as reserve team supremo.

8. Terry Gibson
The diminutive striker is now little to Lawrie Sanchez's large with Northern Ireland.

9. Joe Jordan
Scary centre-forward, these days coaches at Portsmouth.

10. Mike Phelan
The midfielder is now United's first-team coach. He is always in shorts, whatever the weather, when he sits alongside Fergie in the dugout. Is he hoping his number might go up on the subs' board?

11. Clayton Blackmore
Recently plugged his sunbed in at Bangor City.

EMERALD REDS: 11 UNITED IRISHMEN

This all-Ireland team would take some stopping

1. Harry Gregg
Born in Magherafelt. The goalkeeper was one of only a handful of players to emerge from the Munich wreckage unscathed.

2. Denis Irwin
Born in Cork. Quiet, unassuming, brilliant.

3. Ashley Grimes
Born in Dublin. Grimes is immortalised on the mural of Legends, the Old Trafford chip shop; he's the one with the bubble perm nobody recognises.

4. Kevin Moran
Born in Dublin. So hard was Moran that his reflection used to take fright every morning when he went to shave.

5. John O'Shea
Born in Waterford. Johnny is still marching down the wing to chip in the odd cracker.

6. Sammy McIlroy
Born in Belfast. The last Busby Babe.

7. Roy Keane
Born in Cork. The incomparable leader of our football team for more than a decade.

8. Norman Whiteside
Born in Belfast. The Irish Pelé, until injury and Guinness took their toll.

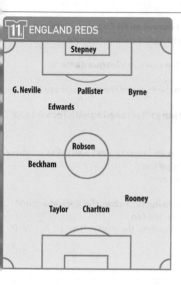

11. ENGLAND REDS

Stepney

G. Neville   Pallister   Byrne

Edwards

Robson

Beckham

Rooney

Taylor   Charlton

Thirty years of hurt might have been greatly diminished if this selection had ever played together for England. Obviously, the formation is a tad skewed.

9. Frank Stapleton
Born in Dublin. An ex-Gooner, but we won't hold that against him.

10. Billy Whelan
Born in Dublin. A goal machine cut down before his prime, in the Munich air disaster.

11. George Best
Born in Belfast. It is all in a name and his said it all.

ERIC EVENTS
Hold the front page, and see inside pages 2–5…

1. Eric arrives from Leeds United in November 1992 for £1m
A Yorkshire entrepreneur is left with a warehouse full of Leeds T-shirts printed with the legend Ooh Aah Cantona.

2. Eric kicks Norwich City's John Polston during an FA Cup tie in February 1994
The referee is looking the other way. Much to Jimmy Hill's annoyance.

3. Eric stamps on John Moncur of Swindon Town in a league game in March 1994 and is sent off
Moncur says he will still vote for Cantona in the Player of the Year award poll.

4. Four days later, Eric is sent off at Highbury after tangling with Tony Adams
The Sun's headline is: "A nutter."

5. Eric is sent off against Crystal Palace on 25 January 1995 and takes a detour to the dressing room via the chest of a lippy fan
The Sun's headline is: "I'll never forget his evil eyes."

6. Eric appears at a press conference following his successful appeal against a two-week jail sentence for the assault on the fan
Asked for a comment he says: "When seagulls follow the trawler they are hoping for sardines to be thrown into the sea."

7. Eric decks journalist Terry Lloyd
The ITN reporter (later to die in Iraq) has followed him to his holiday retreat, where he is trying to relax after being given a record nine-month suspension by the FA.

8. Eric makes his comeback
Thirteen games in Eric's comeback season 1995/96 are decided by Cantona with winners or equalisers.

9. Eric Le Conqueror
On 11 May 1996, Eric becomes first foreign captain to lift the FA Cup.

10. Eric appears in a series of Nike ads
He takes us through his various misdemeanors and then announces that he is surprised that after all that he could find a sponsor. Such is the success of the campaign, he announces he would like to become an actor when he retires from the game.

ERIC LE CONQUEROR, OR "THE NUTTER" ACCORDING TO THE TABLOIDS

11. Eric retires, May 1997
A sad day for English football.

11. v EVERTON 1985

Bailey

Gidman Moran (sent off) McGrath Albiston

Strachan Robson Whiteside Olsen

Stapleton Hughes

18 May 1985
FA Cup final
Wembley.
Manchester United 1
(Whiteside) Everton 0
Big Ron's finest moment,
though one Kevin Moran
would prefer to forget.

EXPENSE-BUSTING TRANSFERS

Just hand over the money

1. **Albert Quixall** £45,000 from Sheffield Wednesday, September 1958
2. **Denis Law** £115,000 from Torino, August 1962
3. **Willie Morgan** £110,000 from Burnley, August 1968
4. **Gordon McQueen** £495,000 from Leeds United, February 1978
5. **Bryan Robson** £1.5m from West Bromwich Albion, October 1981
6. **Gary Pallister** £2.3m from Middlesbrough, August 1989
7. **Roy Keane** £3.75m from Nottingham Forest, July 1993
8. **Andy Cole** £7m from Newcastle United, January 1995
9. **Ruud van Nistelrooy** £19m from PSV Eindhoven, July 2001
10. **Juan Sebastian Veron** £28.1m from Lazio, July 2001
11. **Rio Ferdinand** £29m from Leeds United, July 2002

FA CUP CLASSICS

So now you gonna believe us?

1. Manchester United 2 Arsenal 1 semi-final replay, Villa Park, April 1999
The game that had it all, from Peter Schmeichel's incredible, last-minute penalty save to the Giggs goal – the best-ever by a United player – scored deep into injury time. Fans invade the pitch at the end and the Treble remains on course.

2. Manchester United 1 Bristol City 0 final, Crystal Palace, April 1909
The first FA Cup win for the Reds and the last time Bristol get anywhere near silverware (unless you count the Freight Rover Trophy). As the team return home, 300,000 people line the streets of Manchester to see the Cup paraded.

3. Manchester United 3 Crystal Palace 3 final, Wembley, May 1990
A cracker, with the lead being swapped around more often than Abi Titmuss: Mark Hughes gets two for United, Ian Wright two for Palace. Jim Leighton is blamed for everything, and is dropped for the replay.

4. Manchester United 3 Leicester City 1 final, Wembley, May 1963
Five years after Munich, and at the end of a miserable league season which almost culminates in relegation, a trophy is won at last. Denis Law swivels to score the decisive goal and a dynasty is born.

5. Chelsea 3 Manchester United 5 third round, Stamford Bridge, January 1998
At one point, United are 5-0 up, playing the most compelling football seen for a generation. David Beckham, taunted throughout by Chelsea fans, cups his hands to his ears to mock their attacks on his girlfriend's virtue. Half of the home fans have left by the time Chelsea's three late consolations are scored.

6. Manchester United 2 Liverpool 1 fourth round, Old Trafford, January 1999
The Treble seems a long, long way away as Liverpool lead an off-the-boil United
with barely a minute to go. Then Dwight Yorke equalises, and Ole Gunnar Solskjaer
scores the winner in injury time. It is an uncanny rehearsal of what is to come and
a gleeful Stretford End demand to know: "Who put the ball in the Scousers' net?"

7. Manchester United 2 Arsenal 1 semi-final, Villa Park, April 1983
Bryan Robson and a teenage sensation called Norman Whiteside score to secure
revenge over the Gunners for their last-minute win in the final, four years earlier. The
spirit in the Red ranks is summed up by Kevin Moran who, carried off with a head wound
in the second-half, salutes the United faithful with a clenched fist from the stretcher.

8. Manchester United 4 Brighton 0 final (replay), Wembley, May 1983
Brighton's Gordon Smith seemingly must score in the last minute of the 2-2 drawn
first game but fails to do so. The Seagulls are encouraged to see totemic centre-back
Steve Foster, complete with white head band, returning after suspension for the
replay. "What a difference you have made," the United fans taunt him, as Brighton
go down 4-0 to a rampant Red side.

9. Manchester United 4 Chelsea 0 final, Wembley, May 1994
Ferguson's first Double is achieved in style as Glenn Hoddle's team are hammered
4-0 in monsoon-like rain. Cantona scores two penalties (the first was so unlikely no
United player even appealed). Joining in the fun are Brian McClair and Mark Hughes
(on his way to accumulating a hearty haul of FA Cup winners' medals – he later gets
one more with Chelsea).

10. Manchester United 1 Arsenal 0 semi-final, Villa Park, April 2004
The Gunners are undefeated in the league, playing beautiful football, tipped by
every pundit in London as nailed-on for the Double. But United want it more. In the
stands, Reds' fans urge their team on so enthusiastically, the atmosphere is like
a throwback to the 1970s. Not that Arsène Wenger will have enjoyed it: at times the
abuse he takes from the United sections borders on scandalous.

11. Manchester United 3 Oldham Athletic 3 semi-final, Maine Road, April 1990
Joe Royle's Second Division leaders are dismissed by many as ripe for a walkover.
But inspired by midfielder Mike Milligan's finest hour (he never replicates it when
transferred to City), the Latics are steadfast. Neil Webb, Bryan Robson and Danny
Wallace all score. Oldham match the lot. However, they have nothing left for the
replay and Brian McClair and Mark Robins take United through to the first final of
the Ferguson era.

FAMILIAR FACES

11 Old Trafford players who made it elsewhere

1. David Platt

The one who still has youth-team supremo Eric Harrison waking up nights in a cold sweat, Platt was let go as a youngster by Big Ron in 1986. He moved to Crewe, then on to Villa, Bari, Juventus, Sampdoria, Arsenal and the England captaincy. Might have got the odd game at Old Trafford, then.

2. Johnny Giles

Giles fell out with Matt Busby just before the glory days of the 1960s, and stropped off to Leeds United where he became the foundation of Don Revie's championship-winning side. He was the very definition of the kind of player who is a snide, dirty bastard when playing for someone else, but a hero in your own colours.

3. Peter Beardsley

What was Big Ron doing? Buys the lad from Vancouver Whitecaps in 1982, plays him for half a game then sells him straight back. All this while paying big money for Terry Gibson, Alan Brazil and Peter Davenport.

4. Dion Dublin

Unlucky to break his leg soon after arriving from Cambridge United in 1992, Dublin was let go when Eric Cantona arrived. Went on to provide stalwart service for Aston Villa, Coventry City and Leicester City.

5. Jimmy Rimmer

Youth-team keeper who played 45 times in the first team during Wilf McGuinness's short management tenure. Left for Arsenal in 1974, but his career really blossomed at Aston Villa with whom he won a European Cup winners' medal in 1982 – his second, having been substitute for United in 1968.

> AS A YOUTH-TEAM PLAYER, ROBBIE SAVAGE WAS FOREVER BEING TOLD TO GET HIS HAIR CUT BY FERGIE

6. Don Givens

Elegant Irish forward who won six international caps while on United's books, yet made only eight first-team appearances. Transferred to Luton Town in 1970, he went on to great things with QPR, being the club's leading scorer when they finished First Division runners-up in 1976. His last-ever kick in league football was a penalty he missed for Sheffield United. If he had scored, it would have prevented the Blades from being relegated to Division Four.

7. Robbie Savage

As a youth-team player, the ludicrously coiffured Welshman was forever being told to get his hair cut by Fergie. One of only two players from the great 1992 FA Youth Cup-winning side never to be given a run-out in the first team (the other is George Switzer), he went on to Crewe in 1994, thence to Leicester, Birmingham, Blackburn and the serial loathing of every opposition supporter.

8. John Connelly

Played in the first match of England's 1966 World Cup campaign, and made half a dozen appearances for United after it. Busby sold him to Blackburn that August. He spent another five years patrolling the Ewood Park wings before moving to Bury and then on to run a chip shop in Burnley. Eee, it was all glamour in them days.

9. Jonathan Macken

City's powerful, intelligent centre-forward was sold to Preston in 1998 without ever appearing in the first team. A bag-full of goals at Deepdale persuaded Kevin Keegan to part with £5m to make him a blue, but a series of bad injuries saw his career splutter. Recently back in the Blue first team, where he is obliged to play alongside a short, Scouse potato-impressionist.

10. Danny Webber

Made just one substitute's appearance in the League Cup before he was sold to Watford in 2003 for £250,000. It was money well spent for the Hornets: Webber has been their top scorer ever since.

11. David Johnson

Pacy, strong Brummie forward – and soul mate of Ryan Giggs – Johnson left for Bury in 1995. Ipswich paid £1m for him, then he went to Nottingham Forest for £3m. Injury prevented him ever reaching his full potential.

FERGIE FALL-OUT

11 who have crossed Sir Alex

1. Arsène Wenger

Pizzagate, winegate, tunnelgate and Rooneygate: the spat between the two managers of England's most successful teams of the last decade has been the most entertaining enmity in football. It all began nine years ago, when Arsène Wenger first arrived in England from Japan and refused Fergie's offer of a post-match claret.

Though frankly it is hard to picture the scene. After all, what would an urbane, avuncular sophisticate with a passionate interest in good conversation, music, movies, politics, horse-racing and top Bordeaux vintages find to talk about with a bloke whose idea of a great night is studying Prozone reports of French Second Division reserve teams?

2. Kenny Dalglish

The finest-ever Scottish footballer was manager of Liverpool in 1988 when, after a typically ferocious Manc-Scouse encounter, Fergie suggested that refereeing decisions at Anfield stuck in the throat like vomit. Dalglish, clutching his then infant daughter, was asked for his comment on the visiting manager's observation. "You'd be better off asking the baby, she makes more sense," he responded. The bad blood dated back to Fergie's decision, as Scotland manager, not to take Kenny's pal Alan Hansen to the 1986 World Cup.

3. Alan Hansen

In temporary charge of Scotland for the 1986 World Cup after Jock Stein died mid-qualification, Fergie riled the then Liverpool centre-back by leaving him out of the squad. Hansen, who at the time made José Mourinho look enslaved by self-doubt, was almost as upset as Kenny. Ever since, Fergie has seen every barbed observation on *Match Of The Day* as the extended extraction of revenge.

4. Brian Barwick

The Chief Executive of the FA, and avowed Liverpool fan, was head of sport at the BBC and blamed by Fergie for not giving United the team award in the Sports Review of the Year when they won the Double in 1996. Routinely described ever since as "that bastard", it could make FA disciplinary meetings interesting now Barwick is in charge at Soho Square.

5. Jimmy Hill

The be-chinned one inflamed Fergie by describing United live on the BBC as looking "beaten in the warm-up" before the FA Cup tie against Nottingham Forest in 1990 – the game which changed the Boss's fortunes at the club. So when Hill described Eric Cantona as "despicable and villainous" after a clash with Norwich's John Polston during an FA Cup tie in 1994, Fergie was hardly going to hold back. "If you want a prat, Jimmy Hill is that prat," he fumed.

6. Andrei Kanchelskis

Fergie could never quite work out the Russian international's fragile mental condition, and eventually tired of trying. When Kanchelskis was transferred to

Everton, following all sorts of strange background activity involving highly suspect Russian representatives, he ensured he would never return by saying: "My heart is with United, but I cannot stay for one reason: the manager."

7. Paul Ince
Remembering the treatment he had received from West Ham fans when he signed for United, Paul Ince conducted an assiduous PR campaign among Reds in the summer of 1995 to have the story put about that he did not want to leave United and was being driven out of the club. But when it comes to control of the media, Ferguson is the master. He let it be known that Ince had actively sought a move, holding talks with Internazionale well before that year's FA Cup final. "Big-time Charlie", Fergie called the player, a nickname the Stretford End enjoyed using far more than Ince's own preferred moniker of Guvnor.

8. The BBC (and much of Fleet Street)
The *Daily Mail*, the *Daily Mirror*: anywhere that Ken Lawrence works have often felt the wrong end of Fergie's ire during his time at Old Trafford. But the bannings and temporary exiles many a reporter has endured are nothing compared to his long-time hostility to the Beeb. As if employing Barwick, Hansen, Hill, Alan Green and the rest of what he calls "The Liverpool Supporters' Club" was not enough, the corporation also gave house room to Michael Crick's documentary which raised questions about son Jason's dealings as an agent. *Five Live*, *Match Of The Day* and even the Beeb's Manchester radio station, *GMR*, will all have to get by without direct comment from the top man for the rest of his time at United.

9. Mel Stein
The lawyer-agent turned thriller-writer was blamed by the Boss for the breakdown of Paul Gascoigne's transfer from Newcastle. Ferguson was convinced he had the deal secured; Stein, however, had yet to hear the details of Spurs' terms. Ever since that time, it has not been the best of career moves for any young Manchester United pro to sign up with Stein.

10. John Magnier
Introduced at the Cheltenham Festival in 1997 by the bookie Mike Dillon, Ferguson quickly becomes friends with the Irish racing magnate. Both seem to gain from the relationship: Fergie has a welcome distraction from football, and Magnier has a celebrity to lead his champions round the winners' enclosure. Fergie is thrilled when Magnier buys into United, seeing him as an ally on the board. But in racing there is no such thing as a free lunch, let alone a free half-ownership of a champion. The fall-out over ownership of the Rock of Gibraltar makes the spat between Spain and

Britain over the real thing look cosy. Magnier first causes trouble for Fergie by demanding answers of the plc to 99 questions – several about son Jason's dealings. Then the Irishman cheerfully sells his shares to Glazer, trousering £25m and plunging his former friend's place of employment into misery and uncertainty.

11. Martin Edwards
For years, Fergie backed Edwards, grateful that his boss had stood by him in the dark autumn of 1989, when many a chairman would have panicked and wielded the axe. But, over time, the manager wearied of Edwards's parsimony in contract discussions (particularly when he saw how much the chairman was extracting from the club for himself), and by the end of Edwards's time at Old Trafford the pair were not talking.

FILM AND TV MOMENTS

Hollywood doubtless can't tell its Ronaldos apart, but United have notched up a fair few dramatic appearances on the big and small screen

1. Kes
Ken Loach's 1969 masterpiece includes the funniest football sequence ever committed to celluloid. During a games lesson, Brian Glover as the PE teacher insists his team are United and he is Bobby Charlton (Denis Law, apparently, is in the wash). Much of the movie was improvised and Glover is clearly having the time of his life. Watch it and weep.

2. Bend It Like Beckham
Gurinder Chada's story of a young Asian female footballer obsessed with the boy David just wouldn't have been the same had he been at Real Madrid at the time.

3. The Day After Tomorrow
As the world freezes over in this bombastic disaster story, a scientist in a remote weather station is watching United play Celtic in a Champions League game on the telly. Since they have never met in the competition, someone in the graphics department must have had a lot of fun painting in the green stripes.

4. Cracker
In the most chilling episode of Robbie Coltrane's turn as a forensic psychologist, a traumatised Hillsborough survivor-turned-serial killer (played by Robert Carlisle) turns up in the United section at Old Trafford, supporting Liverpool. Memorably told to piss off and rob some cars by a home fan.

5. Coronation Street
Curly Watts and his City fixation and Roy's Leicester City allusions were a diversion. The Street reflects the real Manchester: it has long been painted red, red and red.

6. Best
The most entertaining aspect of this 2000 biopic of the sainted George is the cast. Jerome Flynn (of Robson and… fame) is Bobby Charlton. Ian Hart (who later played hostage Brian Keenan) is Nobby Stiles and – quite bizarrely – Roger Daltrey of The Who is Rodney Marsh. Ian Bannen, playing a Matt Busby so prone to philosophical turns of phrase he appears to have been scripted by Confucius, looks like a living-dead Soviet leader.

7. Cup Fever
The real Busby (as well as Charlton, Law and Stiles) turns up in this Children's Film Foundation Saturday matinee from 1965. A kids' team called Barton United are threatened with closure by a nasty councillor (Bernard Cribbins). Their local club – which happens to be Manchester United – steps in to save the day.

8. Ball Of Fortune
Only a fragment of this 1926 silent film survives, but what a fragment: Billy Meredith dancing down the wing at Elland Road, a collection of Leeds players floundering in his wake.

9. From Jemapoh To Manchester
Malaysia's biggest cinema hit in 1998, this is the tale of two young lads who steal a red Volvo and set off from their rural village to fulfil their greatest ambition – seeing a football match in Manchester. Let's face it, they weren't prepared to drive all that way to watch City.

10. Manchester United Ruined My Life
TV version of bitter blue Colin Schindler's book concludes with Nick Hancock as a psychiatrist giving a lengthy rant about how much he hates Eric Cantona. To paraphrase the biblical instruction: psychiatrist cure thyself.

11. The Simpsons
When the Springfield five visit England, Homer becomes obsessed with football and tells Marge how outraged he is that Ryan Giggs is not awarded a penalty in a match he has just watched. Never mind a knighthood for Sir Alex or Sir Matt: a name-check by the great yellow philosopher is the highest honour ever bestowed on a Red.

FLOPS

Cue the ironic applause

1. Garry Birtles
Recycled jokes number 65. The first thing American hostages asked when released from Iran in 1981 was 'Has Birtles scored yet?' The club's £1.25m record signing from Forest played 25 games in his first season and didn't score once. After 12 goals in 64 appearances he was sold back to Forest for £275,000.

2. Ralph Milne
Still portrayed as a tragi-comic figure by United fans, Milne was a decent winger with Dundee United. He then found his true level playing with Second Division Bristol City before Fergie swooped like an eagle chasing a wild boar.

3. Diego Forlan
Forlan's Birtles-like start to a United career stuck with him and for £7m, United fans expected more than ten goals in 62 matches. Now scoring for fun in Spain with Villareal. It was always going to happen.

4. Juan Sebastian Veron
Outstanding in some games (usually European ones), anonymous in others. Reds were not being unreasonable in hoping for more for £28.1m. Now back on form with Internazionale.

5. Colin Gibson
The fitness fanatic who played left-back in the Aston Villa side which won the league and European Cup. It wasn't his fault his time at United didn't work out; the club's doctors never diagnosed his cruciate injury. Leicester's did…

6. Nikola Jovanovic
United's first foreign signing in 1980. He came, he saw and he buggered off back to Belgrade after 25 games. With his club BMW.

7. Eric Djemba Djemba
Cost the same as Roy Keane. That's where the comparisons end.

8. Neil Webb
Classy after signing from Nottingham Forest in 1989; less than spectacular after picking up an injury on international duty a month after becoming a Red. More recently, cruelly exposed by *The Sun* for the heinous crime of being a postman.

9. Terry Gibson
The moustached, pot-noodle-sized striker cost £630,000 in 1986 and scored once before leaving for Wimbledon for £200,000. Do the maths: £630,000 for one goal...

10. Ted MacDougall
An expensive panic buy from Bournemouth in September 1972. The words "United" and "Not good enough to play for" were regularly used in close proximity as he slunk back south to West Ham five months later.

11. George Graham
Losing your place is one thing, losing it in a season when your side is relegated, as Stroller did in 1973/74, is more damning.

(WE ALL) FOLLOW UNITED

11 top away followings (excluding domestic cup finals and semi-finals)

1. **55,000 out of 90,000** Barcelona, May 1999
2. **26,000/45,000** Rotterdam, May 1991
3. **25,000/30,115** Wimbledon, May 1993
4. **25,000/38,152** Bolton Wanderers, March 1975
5. **19,000/26,384** Oldham Athletic, December 1974
6. **18,000/48,105** Sheffield Wednesday, November 1985
7. **17,000/25,370** Blackpool, October 1974
8. **17,000/54,161** Arsenal, February 1988
9. **16,000/44,184** Chelsea, May 1973
10. **13,000/21,055** Notts County, January 1991
11. **12,000/24,429** Coventry City, April 1993

FOOTBALLERS OF THE YEAR

Reds only need apply...

1. **Johnny Carey** Football Writers' Association Player of the Year, 1949
2. **Denis Law** European Footballer of the Year, 1964
3. **Bobby Charlton** FWA and European Footballer of the Year, 1966
4. **George Best** FWA and European Footballer of the Year, 1968
5. **Mark Hughes** PFA Player of the Year, 1989 and 1991

6. **Lee Sharpe** PFA Young Footballer of the Year, 1991
7. **Gary Pallister** PFA Player of the Year, 1992
8. **Eric Cantona** PFA Player of the Year, 1994; FWA Player of the Year, 1996
9. **Roy Keane** FWA and PFA Player of the Year, 2000
10. **Teddy Sheringham** FWA and PFA Player of the Year, 2001
11. **Ruud van Nistelrooy** PFA Player of the Year 2002

GREATEST GOALS

United's finest, from the 1960s to the present. We allowed one goal only per player, arranged them alphabetically (you *can't* pick an order here) and, yes, very nearly included Schmeichel's injury-time strike against Rotor Volgograd

1. David Beckham v Wimbledon August 1996

The moment Beckham becomes A-list. Having seen Jordi Cruyff almost chip the Wimbledon keeper Neil Sullivan from outside the box, Beckham thinks he'll do likewise from his own half. He looks up briefly, then the ball sails high through the Croydon sky before coming to earth in the Wimbledon net. Poor Sullivan is condemned to watch himself sprawling in the back of the net in endless television documentaries about the Beckham phenomenon.

> THE BALL SAILS HIGH THROUGH THE CROYDON SKY. BECKHAM HAS BECOME A-LIST

2. George Best v Benfica European Cup quarter-final, Lisbon, March 1966

Benfica were the sharpest team in Europe but Best, at 19, was the sharpest teenager in football. His second goal in a 5-1 rout, dancing and weaving through the Portuguese defence, so entranced the locals they called him El Beatle. After the flight home, Best, with an eye for a photo opportunity, wore a huge sombrero as he sauntered down the steps of the plane. The footballer as pop star was born.

3. Eric Cantona v Sunderland December 1995
Collecting the ball just inside the Mackems' half, Eric outmanoeuvres two opponents before playing a one-two with Brian McClair. Cantona looks up briefly, then chips the ball over advancing keeper Lionel Perez. While others might have dashed round half the pitch in celebration, Cantona stands motionless, hands on hips, surveying all around him. "Cantona the conductor of the United cantata," is the headline in the *Independent*.

4. Bobby Charlton v Benfica European Cup final, Wembley, May 1968
It's the long-range blockbusters you recall when Sir Bobby is mentioned: the iconic models for all those later screamers from Beckham, Scholes and latterly, Rooney. But Sir Bobby's most important, most emotional goals were in the great Benfica final. His first, the opener, was a collector's item – a header. But we opt for his second, United's fourth. Brian Kidd crosses the ball, Bobby – looking drained to the bones in extra time – runs onto it and rockets its trajectory, on, at the tightest of angles. The great dream is finally very, very real.

5. Ryan Giggs v Arsenal FA Cup semi-final replay, Villa Park, April 1999
Giggs intercepts a pass from Patrick Vieira in his own half well into extra time, then begins a mazy dribble around and through five Arsenal players before thundering a shot past David Seaman. His strip-tease celebration exposes enough chest hair to make David Hasselhoff envious. United go through to the final, with Ferguson proclaiming: "There is not a player in the world to touch Giggs in that form." Vieira has admitted the goal still haunts him to this day.

6. Mark Hughes v Barcelona Cup Winners' Cup final, Rotterdam, 15 May 1991
Maybe it's a fraction offside, but Hughes's second goal against Barcelona is one of his best, a fierce volley from an implausible angle that, according to Ferguson, "left their goalkeeper picking daisies somewhere".

7. Denis Law v Burnley Old Trafford, September 1966
Law, the King of Old Trafford, was the most elegant goalpoacher that ever graced English football, popping up to score in the box with a flick of the head, a poke of the toe, even that awful back heel for City. He is one of the players who has been credited with introducing the bicycle kick – he saw it while playing in Italy – to these shores, and this acrobatic goal was a classic. Pat Crerand slips the ball to Best, who eludes a couple of defenders before stumbling to the ground where, incredibly, he still manages to flick the ball goalwards. Law, back to the goal, is not to be outdone and launches himself into a perfect overhead.

8. Bryan Robson v Liverpool FA Cup semi-final replay (Maine Road) April 1985
A goal down at Maine Road, Robson exchanges passes with Frank Stapleton on the half-way line then runs towards the Liverpool goal. The pursuing Scouse defenders seem close, until Robson unleashes a shot that flies past Bruce Grobbelaar.

9. Wayne Rooney v Newcastle United April 2005
United are lacklustre and no one can see where a goal is coming from. When they get a free kick, deep in their own half, Rooney trails the referee upfield, having a moan, then looks up to see the ball headed into his path by the Newcastle defence. He thunders a 30-yard volley into the top corner, a shot so strong that Sky replay it for the viewers to *listen* to the thump of boot against ball. Amazingly, after the match, it turns out the boy wonder had a dead leg at the time of his strike, and was just about to be substituted.

10. Ole Gunnar Solskjaer v Bayern Munich Champions League final (Barcelona) May 1999
He put the ball in the Germans' net. It was only a toe-poke, an instinctive prod from a player who should never have got near the ball if the defenders had been doing their job properly and marked him. But be honest, is there any other goal that has produced a reaction like that?

11. Norman Whiteside v Everton FA Cup final (Wembley) May 1985
Down to ten men against champions Everton after Kevin Moran becomes the first man to be sent off in an FA Cup final, United ought to be beaten. Instead the 78th-minute expulsion spurs Ron Atkinson's men on. In extra time, Mark Hughes passes to Whiteside wide on the right wing; he runs into the area, sells Pat van der Hauwe a Ronaldo-style step-over, then curls a deceptive shot past Neville Southall.

GREATEST VICTORIES
You must remember these

1. Manchester United 2 Bayern Munich 1 May 1999
Solskjaer and Sheringham's late, great show in the Champions League final.

2. Manchester 4 Benfica 1 May 1968
Three extra-time goals and United become the first English team to win the European Cup.

3. Juventus 2 Manchester United 3 April 1999
The Roy Keane show. With support from Andy Cole and Dwight Yorke at their most compelling.

4. Benfica 1 Manchester United 5 March 1966
The match when George Best dazzled the Stadium of Light.

5. Manchester United 3 Barcelona 0 March 1984
The Catalans, complete with Maradona, had won the first leg of this Cup Winners' Cup quarter-final 2-0. United stormed back and beat them 3-0 at Old Trafford. Many fans say it's the best atmosphere they've experienced.

6. Manchester United 2 Liverpool 1 May 1977
The Scousers were going for the Treble and needed to beat United in the FA Cup final. They didn't.

7. Arsenal 4 Manchester United 5 February 1958
The last domestic game before Munich. What a send-off.

8. Newton Heath 5 Ardwick 1 October 1891
The first derby (Ardwick were to become City) takes place in the FA Cup qualifying round. And City fans think they have possession of that particular scoreline...

9. Manchester United 10 Anderlecht 0 September 1956
Played at Maine Road, because Old Trafford didn't yet have floodlights.

10. Manchester United 3 Sheffield Wednesday 0 February 1958
With a blank team-sheet in the programme, United were carried forward on a wave of emotion after Munich.

11. Arsenal 2 Manchester United 6
November 1990
A remarkable result against the champions who were unbeaten at home in over a year. Lee Sharpe scored three and did his famous celebratory Elvis impression.

> UNITED'S CLASH WITH JUVENTUS IN 1999 SHOULD BE DUBBED 'THE ROY KEANE SHOW'

HARDMEN

We'll see you outside

1. Duncan Edwards 1952-58
Though the Munich air casualty is generally celebrated for his artistry, the man-child was already so scary at 15 that grown men would shrink in the tackle.

2. Tommy Taylor 1953-58
An ex-pitman of a centre-forward, all elbows, knees and a forehead hewn from Yorkshire granite.

3. Nobby Stiles 1960-71
Collyhurst embodied. As uncompromising in pursuit of the ball as he was mild-mannered and uncomplicated off the pitch.

4. Pat Crerand 1963-71
Born into the green side of the Glasgow, only those in urgent pursuit of a new nose would suggest to Pat that he join you in a singalong of *The Billy Boys*.

5. Bryan Robson 1981-94
So frail as a teenager he was fattened up on Guinness and milk, Captain Marvel launched into the fray with bravery that bordered on the self-destructive.

6. Remi Moses 1981-88
It's the quiet ones you need to worry about, and Moses never said a word.

7. Norman Whiteside 1981-89
Though graced with a left foot that could inspire poetry, when the mood took him Whiteside was about as subtle and refined as his nickname: the Shankhill skinhead.

11. HARD MEN: DON'T MESS

Schmeichel

Keane   Stam   Stiles   Heinze

Robson   Whiteside   Crerand

Cantona

Hughes   Taylor

To devise a workable formation, some of the hard men in the list had to be sacrificed. Obviously we'd need someone truly hard – Sir Alex? – to tell messrs Stiles and Edwards they weren't in the final XI.

8. Mark Hughes 1983-86 and 1988-95
Sparky stamped and snorted like something let loose on the streets of Pamplona. Asking a defender to stop him was the equivalent of suggesting they step in a tumble drier with a load of cement.

9. Gary Pallister 1989-98
John Fashanu reckoned that there was just one player that the Wimbledon crazy gang could never intimidate in the tunnel before a game, and that was Dolly. Or was it Daisy?

10. Nicky Butt 1992-2004
Some found glory in goals, others enjoyed the flash of the photographers' studios, but one member of the class of 1992 liked nothing better than destroying opposition attacks.

11. Roy Keane 1993-
Even 6ft 4in, square-shouldered French tough guys soon shut up when Keano gets involved.

EVEN TALL FRENCH TOUGH GUYS SHUT UP WHEN KEANO GETS INVOLVED

HAT-TRICK HEROES

That ball is mine…

1. Jack Rowley v Swansea Town December 1937
At 17 years 58 days Rowley became the youngest player to record a United hat-trick, then added a fourth for good measure.

2. Charlie Mitten v Aston Villa March 1950
One for the pub quiz: Mitten scores four, including a hat-trick of penalties.

3. George Best v Northampton Town FA Cup, February 1970
Best scores six on his return from suspension.

4. Andy Ritchie v Leeds United March 1979
The lad scores three and is dropped for the next match. A year later, he scores three against Spurs and is once again promptly dropped.

5. Lee Sharpe v Arsenal League Cup, November 1990
Sharpe notches three in a 6–2 rout, Arsenal's worst home defeat in 50 years.

6. Andrei Kanchelskis v Manchester City November 1994
The Ukrainian speed-merchant scores three as United exorcise 1989's 5–1 defeat by winning 5–0.

7. Andy Cole v Ipswich Town March 1995
Cole bags five in a record Premiership 9–0 win.

8. Ole Gunnar Solskjaer v Nottingham Forest February 1999
Four goals in 13 minutes as a substitute is a club record likely to endure.

9. Ruud van Nistelrooy v Fulham March 2003
Ruud records his first hat-trick for the club, including what he reckons is his best goal, a powerful run and dribble from the half-way line.

10. Wayne Rooney v Fenerbahce Champions League, September 2004
The kid scores three crackers on his United debut.

11. Denis Law v the World
Law was the king of hat-tricks, scoring 18 of them in total, including seven in the 1963/64 season alone.

HEAVYWEIGHTS
A goalie-heavy collection of sizeable talents

1. **15st 13lb** Peter Schmeichel, goalkeeper (1991–99)
2. **14st 13lb** Gary Pallister, defender (1989–98)
3. **14st 13lb** Gary Walsh, goalkeeper (1986–95)
4. **14st 4lb** Caesar Augustus Llewelyn Jenkins, defender (1896–98)
5. **14st 1lb** Jaap Stam, defender (1998–2001)
6. **13st 12lb** Gary Bailey, goalkeeper (1978–86)
7. **13st 11lb** Eric Cantona, God (1992–97)
8. **13st 9lb** Gordon Clayton, goalkeeper (1956–57)
9. **13 lb 8lb** Les Sealey, goalkeeper (1989–90)
10. **13st 8lb** Gordon McQueen, defender (1978–85)
11. **13st 7lb** Mark Bosnich, goalkeeper (1989–91 and 1999–2000)

!HOLAS!
Reds who moved to the sun

1. Stuart Pearson
Pancho lives on the Costa Del Sol but still returns to do corporate hospitality.

2. Mark Hughes
Left for Barça in 1986. His Spanish didn't get past the 'dos cervezas por favor' stage.

3. Diego Forlan
Profligacy pays... Forlan got a pay rise when he joined Villareal.

4. Brian Greenhoff
Menorca is now the home to the 1970s defender.

5. John Gidman
The raffish 1980s right-back lives near Marbella.

6. Kevin Moran
Left United for Sporting Gijon in evergreen Asturias.

7. Peter Barnes
The son of the man who scouted Giggs for City had a year in Seville with Real Betis.

> SOLSKJAER'S FOUR GOALS IN 13 MINUTES AS A SUB IS A RECORD LIKELY TO ENDURE

8. Ricardo
No surprise the former Valladolid goalkeeper lived in Spain. He is Spanish, after all.

9. Ashley Grimes
The bubble-permed 1980s midfielder ran with the bulls of Osasuna in Pamplona for two years.

10. Quinton Fortune
When he told his team-mates in Atletico Madrid's reserve team that he was joining Manchester United they thought he was joking.

11. David Beckham
Didn't he go off to join some Spanish team?

HOME ADVANTAGE

11 all-time highest average attendances of English clubs (since 1945)

1. **67,641** Manchester United 2003/04
2. **67,630** Manchester United 2002/03
3. **67,586** Manchester United 2001/02
4. **67,544** Manchester United 2000/01
5. **58,017** Manchester United 1999/2000
6. **57,759** Manchester United 1967/68
7. **56,283** Newcastle United 1947/48
8. **55,509** Tottenham Hotspur 1950/51
9. **55,188** Manchester United 1998/99
10. **55,168** Manchester United 1997/98
11. **55,080** Manchester United 1996/97

ASHLEY GRIMES TOOK HIS BUBBLE-PERMED HAIR AND WENT OFF TO RUN WITH THE BULLS

IN A PARALLEL UNIVERSE

11 things you didn't know about the other Manchester United – in Gibraltar

1. They were league champions in 1999 too

Yes, they finished the season four points ahead of Glacis United in the first level of the Gibraltar league. Their reserves didn't do quite as well – finishing sixth (out of eight) in the second level.

2. But they haven't won the league since...

They finished 20 points behind Newcastle in 2004/05 – not a scenario that's likely to be repeated in the Premiership any time soon.

3. They can't enter the Champions League

Or any other European competition for that matter. Gibraltar's application to join UEFA has been officially pending for at least two years now. The disputed status of this lump of limestone rock means that Gibraltarian sides can only play foreign teams in friendlies.

4. They asked Sir Matt if they could use the Manchester United name

Sir Matt Busby, being a generous soul, wrote back, telling them to go ahead and so Manchester United Gibraltar was born in 1962.

5. They have enjoyed periods of domestic dominance

Although not quite as successful of late, they reigned supreme on the Rock from 1975 to 1984, winning the league in 1975, 1979, 1980 and 1984, and winning the Rock Cup in 1974, 1977 and 1980.

6. They are two divisions above Chelsea

In 2003/04, Gibraltar's Chelsea FC were fourth from the bottom of Division Three.

7. They changed their name to please a sponsor
The days of Manchester United Eurobet were, thankfully, short-lived.

8. They won the Supercup in 2003
Despite only having six clubs in the top flight, Gibraltar has its own equivalent of the Charity Shield called the Pepe Reyes Super Cup, contested by the champions and the winners of the Rock Cup. In 2003 Manchester United beat Newcastle 4-3 in the penalty shoot-out. Even in Gibraltar, Newcastle can't win a shoot-out.

9. They have fewer fans in Gibraltar than you know who...
The Gibraltar branch of the Manchester United fan club has 300 members. The local side of the same name is pleased if 200 fans turn up to watch a game.

10. They have ten teams
All the way from Under-7s up to the 15-player first-team squad which plays its home games at Victoria Stadium. The reserves won the Rock Cup in 1974.

11. They've never played the other Manchester United

IS THAT ENTIRELY WISE?

11 off-pitch dramas that merited a red card

1. Roger Byrne and Duncan Edwards 1957
Who said the Babes were saints? Skipper Byrne crashes his car on the way to training... into the garden wall at Matt Busby's place. Meanwhile Edwards is stopped by police one night on the way home from his girlfriend's house. His crime? Riding his bike without lights. He is fined ten shillings.

2. Remi Moses exacts revenge 1984
In the absence of a referee during a training session, Remi Moses decides to ensure justice is done after he's fouled by Jesper Olsen. Rather than a yellow card, Olsen gets 11 stitches in an eye wound. "It is just one of those things," the Dane says later.

3. Taxi for Paul McGrath 1987
A not entirely sober Paul McGrath crashes his car through not one, not two, but three gardens on his way home from a night out with Bryan Robson and Norman Whiteside. The motor finally comes to a halt in a garden pond. Finding him sprawled across the bonnet, covered in blood, paramedics at the scene assume he is dead.

One of them is about to put a blanket over the body when McGrath opens his eyes and asks someone to call him a cab. "I've got to get back," he explains. "I've got training tomorrow."

4. Lee Sharpe's party 1992
Fergie arrives at Lee Sharpe's house where Ryan Giggs is among the guests. Sensing that the party might be over, everyone heads for the exit, where the boss is waiting to give them each a clip round the ear.

5. Mickey Thomas's bum deal 1993
Mickey is enjoying the company of his ex-wife's sister in the back of his car when her husband turns up and stabs him repeatedly in the buttocks with a screwdriver. "You could have killed me," shrieks Thomas when the assault finally runs out of steam. "That was the idea," comes the response.

6. Nicky Butt's butt (alleged) 1993
Butt is charged with assault after Peter Oldbury, Butt's then girlfriend's ex-boyfriend, claims the midfielder followed him into the gents at Charlie Chan's restaurant in Manchester and, appropriately enough, butted him. Oldbury takes to wearing an eye patch to cover his injuries. The case collapses and Butt is acquitted.

7. Watch those clubs, Lee 1993
Sharpey is attacked by several youths at Coco Savannas, Stockport, after – would you believe it – a disagreement over a woman. He explains that the two black eyes he sports to next day's training were caused in a golfing accident.

8. Mark Hughes's insulting language 1994
Hughes is decked by a bouncer as he leaves Manchester's Hacienda Club after a night out. The doorman clearly doesn't understand that Sparky's apparently racist remark to companion Paul Ince is an ironic commentary on insults allegedly made by Stuart Pearce in a recent game against Forest. Rather than explain the sub-text, or indeed thank a brother for showing solidarity, Ince bawls at the bouncer: "He's my mate, he can call me what he wants!"

9. Martin Edwards, ladies' man 2001
Edwards enters the ladies at Mottram Hall, the Cheshire golf club much favoured by Manchester's monied classes. Worried he might have made a mistake, the United chairman peers under the doors of several occupied cubicles to check the sex of those within. His sense of direction must be wayward as it is the fourth time he has made such an error. In a week. He is asked to resign quietly from the United board.

10. Roy Keane is innocent 2004
Keano is arrested over an alleged assault of a youth during an argument about dog walking. He is cleared at the trial.

11. George Best 1964-2005
It would take several dozen books to detail George Best's scrapes. And he has written several dozen which do just that.

JINDINCHUV-HRADEC AND OTHER RED BIRTHPLACES

Just as all of us Red fans come from Basingstoke, half our players were born in Burma, or indeed Jindinchuv-Hradec. Here are 11 of the wilder shores

1. Barnsley, Yorkshire
Busby Babes Tommy Taylor and Mark Jones, plus the Greenhoff brothers, Brian and Jimmy, all hailed from this gritty Yorkshire town. So, too, did Billy Wrigglesworth, whose war-interrupted career produced ten goals in 37 appearances between 1937 and 1947.

2. Liverpool, Lancashire
The other giant of the north-west was the birthplace of John Gidman, Steve Coppell, Ron Atkinson and Wayne Rooney.

3. Cork, Ireland
The European Capital of Culture 2005 is the birthplace of Roy Keane, Liam Miller, Denis Irwin and Noel Cantwell – who, in 1960, became Britain's most expensive full-back when he was bought by Matt Busby from West Ham United.

4. Hamilton, Canada
The birthplace of 1970s/80s defender Jimmy Nicholl.

5. Aberdeen, Grampian
Classy defender Martin Buchan and goalscoring favourite Denis Law were both born in the Granite City. As were Alex Dawson, John Fitzpatrick, Graeme Hogg, Ian Moir and 1930s star George Mutch.

6. Newcastle, Tyneside
Toon Reds include Steve Bruce, Peter Beardsley, goalkeeper Ray Wood and Joe Spence (who made over 500 United appearances). And Bryan Robson is also of Geordie stock.

7. Peshawar, Pakistan
This historic city, lying at the edge of the Khyber Pass, is where George 'Cocky' Hunter, United's half-back before World War 1, was born.

8. Motherwell (or close by), Lanarkshire
Joe Jordan, Brian McClair, Jimmy Delaney, Arthur Graham, George Graham, Jack Picken, Tom Reid, David Herd, Charlie Rennox, Jim Holton, Harry McShane and Francis Burns. And Sir Matt Busby.

9. Edinburgh, Scotland
Arthur Albiston, Darren Fletcher, Lou Macari and Gordon Strachan.

10. Rangoon, Burma
Charlie Mitten could have played for Burma. He was born there when his dad, a boxer in the British Army, was posted in Rangoon.

11. Jindinchuv-Hradec, Czech Republic
Well, where else did you expect Karel Poborsky to come from? Stoke?

CHARLIE MITTEN WAS BORN IN RANGOON. HIS DAD, A BOXER IN THE BRITISH ARMY, WAS POSTED THERE

KEANO MOMENTS

He really did replace Bryan Robson...

1. The City Ground March 1992
A minute into the start of the game Forest player Keane goes for a 50/50 ball with Bryan Robson. He clatters Robson and wins the ball. Fergie later said: "I couldn't believe the cheek of it." But he had marked Keane's card.

2. His place, Nottingham July 1993
Roy agrees to join Blackburn Rovers for £4 m. He calls Ewood Park on Friday afternoon only to find the offices are closed and he is told to wait until Monday to sign the contract. That weekend Alex Ferguson makes contact. Kenny Dalglish is furious at Keane's subsequent change of mind and threatens to sue him for every penny he has. He doesn't.

3. Maine Road November 1993
Galatasaray have knocked United out of Europe three days previously, and City fans shower the players with Turkish delight in the warm-up. City are 2–0 up at half-time. Cantona scores twice, then Denis Irwin puts a cross behind the City defenders and Keane, having timed his run perfectly, puts the ball away with a half-volley – 3-2.

4. Mayfield, Cork 1997
Roy marries Theresa with just 15 immediate family members in attendance. No photos of the wedding appear in *OK* or *Hello!*.

5. Champions League semi-final, Turin April 1999
Keano's finest hour. Two-nil down against Juventus, the team perceived to be the best in Europe, a Keane-inspired United fight back to win 3-2. Roy gets booked for his troubles and misses the final. His Herculean effort is still regarded by many Reds as the greatest individual performance they've ever seen. Roy reckons he did "alright".

6. Old Trafford March 2000

With the score 0-0 against Middlesbrough, United need a win. Referee Andy D'Urso awards a penalty to Boro. Keane disputes the decision and charges towards the referee, the veins in his forehead bulging. D'Urso keeps retreating; Keane keeps advancing, an image wired around the world. Keane later says: "The photographs were shocking. The psycho in them was me. I know we were wrong, and I was the worst offender."

7. Old Trafford October 2000

After a Champions League tie against Dynamo Kiev, played in a dire atmosphere, Keane says: "Our fans away from home are as good as any, but at home you sometimes wonder if they understand the game of football. Some people come to Old Trafford and I don't think they can even spell the word football, let alone understand it. Away from home our fans are fantastic, what I would call the hard-core fans, but at home they've had a few drinks and probably their prawn sandwiches and don't realise what is going on out on the pitch. It's right out of order."

8. Munich April 2001

After defeat in the Champions League, Keane tells a journalist that the present team "are not good enough. Maybe we need to break it up, get new players, start again". The first of the "Keane Slams Team Mates" headlines is born. What they didn't point out was that he was including himself as being in that comfort zone.

9. Hale August 2002

The media are camping outside chez Keane following his early, unscheduled departure from the World Cup. Most other celebrities would stay in their ivory towers. Not Roy. His wife says: "The dog hasn't been out for a couple of days." So he walks the dog, chased by a pack of unfit journalists whom he ignores. "I thought Triggs was going to bite some of them," says Roy later.

10. Highbury February 2005

Roy accuses 6ft 4in Patrick Vieira of trying to intimidate 5ft 11in Gary Neville in the tunnel before the game. Roy intervenes and tells Vieira in his tender Cork patois to pick on someone his own size. Like him, for instance. Roy is the same height as Gary Neville. Roy goes on to be the man of a match, described by Sir Alex as the best the Premiership has ever seen.

11. St Mary's Stadium, Southampton May 2005

Unused sub Roy is cooling down on the pitch when he is abused by Saints fans after United have sent their team down. In response he points in the direction their club is heading. Enraged, some home fans complain to the police. Poor, sensitive lambs.

LEAGUE SUCCESSES

United's most successful seasons. This table is devised using the old system of two points for a league win. Rankings are according to the total percentage of points gained. Goal difference is used to separate seasons

	Season	P	W	D	L	F	A	Pts	%
1.	1999/00	38	28	7	3	97	45	63	82
2.	1993/94	42	27	11	4	80	38	65	77
3.	2002/03	38	25	8	5	74	34	58	76
4.	1956/57	42	28	8	6	103	54	64	76
5.	1998/99	38	22	13	3	80	37	57	75
6.	1995/96	38	25	7	6	73	35	57	75
7.	2000/01	38	24	8	6	79	31	56	73
8.	1964/65	42	26	9	7	89	39	61	72
9.	1966/67	42	24	12	6	84	45	60	71
10.	1992/93	42	24	12	6	67	31	60	71
11.	1955/56	42	25	10	7	83	51	60	71

LIT CRIT: RED AUTOBIOGRAPHIES

There have been many but here are 11 notables (George Best gets his own section)

1. Roy Keane Keane: The Autobiography, 2002
The peerless United tale by the peerless midfielder, Keane's book has sold more copies in Ireland than any other book except the Bible. Gripping from the start, the prose, crafted by Ireland's best-known journalist Eamon Dunphy, is charged and brutally honest.

2. Sir Alex Ferguson Managing My Life, My Autobiography, 1999
Released a couple of months after the Treble, the timing couldn't have been better.
Nor could Ferguson's choice of Hugh McIlvanney as his ghost writer. A number one
bestseller for months, Fergie's tome is forthright and revealing. Not that Brian Kidd
would, or should, agree.

3. Jaap Stam Head to Head, 2001
Was this the first autobiography which led to a player being sold? Dutch frankness
might work in Maastricht, but not in Manchester where Sir Alex Ferguson's hawk
eyes survey all. Oddly, despite the headlines, it's an insipid read and a bit of
a publishing flop. All in all, not worth Jaap risking his new kitchen installation.

4. Dwight Yorke Dwight Yorke, 1999
An authorised biography by Hunter Davies sounded like a good idea. To people
who'd never met Dwight. Esteemed author Davies, buoyed by a healthy advance,
put the hours in and travelled to Tobago to meet Yorke's family and friends. They
were all happy to talk openly, unlike a totally uninterested Dwight. Davies's writing is
engaging, but it doesn't compensate for Yorke's guard being higher than the list of
notches on his bed post.

5. Nobby Stiles After The Ball, 2003
A beautifully ghosted autobiography by James Lawton, this is the story of a working
class hero told vividly, from Collyhurst trouble and strife, to *This Is Your Life*. Back in
the 1960s, Nobby also published the rather splendidly-titled *Soccer My Battlefield*.

6. Harry Gregg Harry's Game, 2002
Don't be put off by his old-school mindset (Gregg admits he is a modern-day Victor
Meldrew). His description of the Munich air crash, in which the United goalkeeper
rescued others, is more visceral than any other.

7. Denis Law various
The King of the Stretford End has almost as many books to his name as Best. Almost.
Law's 1969 *Book Of Soccer* must have sold well, his 1979 autobiography too, because
decades after he'd finished playing, Law brought out another autobiography in
1999. And then another in 2003.

8. Norman Whiteside My Memories Of Manchester United, 2003
This story of growing up on Belfast's Shankill Road and playing for club and country
while your mates are still at school should have been a great one. Yet Whiteside didn't
want to say a bad word about anyone. So why write a book in the first place?

11. v LIVERPOOL 1977

Stepney

Nicholl B. Greenhoff Buchan Albiston

Coppell McIlroy Macari Hill

J. Greenhoff Pearson

21 May 1977
FA Cup final,
Wembley.
Manchester United 2 (Pearson,
J Greenhoff) Liverpool 1 (Case).
Tommy Docherty's only trophy
at United stops Liverpool
clinching the Treble.

9. Eric Cantona My Story, 1993
Originally published in France under the title *Un Rêve Modeste Et Fou* (literally,
A Dream Modest and Mad), Cantona's life story was translated into English by
George Scanlan, his interpreter at Old Trafford. Given the rich subject matter, Eric is
unusually reticent – perhaps because he'd been at Old Trafford for less than a year.

10. Mark Hughes Sparky: Barcelona, Bayern & Back, 1989
Possibly the worst United player autobiography to hit the printing presses (and
there is stiff competition even for a place on the bench). A hardback containing just
96 pages, Hughes is as insightful in print as Peter Schmeichel is in a television studio.

11. Eric Djemba Djemba So Good They Named
Me Twice, 2005
OK, we lied about this one.

DESPITE STIFF
COMPETITION HUGHES
SUCCEEDED IN
WRITING THE WORST
AUTOBIOGRAPHY

LONGEST-SERVING UNITED MANAGERS

Sir Alex has another five years to go, if he's going to take this record, too...

1. **Sir Matt Busby** 1945-69 and 1970-71
2. **Sir Alex Ferguson** 1986-t
3. **J. Ernest Mangall** 1903-12
4. **Walter Crickmer** 1931-32 and 1937-45
5. **John Robson** 1914-21
6. **Tommy Docherty** 1972-77
7. **Scott Duncan** 1932-37
8. **Ron Atkinson** 1981-86
9. **John Champman** 1921-26
10. **Herbert Bamlett** 1927-31
11. **Dave Sexton** 1977-81, though it might have seemed longer

MAGNIFICO

The top 11 continental Reds

1. Eric Cantona
Better than Best? Some might say. Non?

2. Ruud van Nistelrooy
A goal a game keeps the long face happy.

3. Peter Schmeichel
What did you expect from someone born in Gladsaxe?

4. Jaap Stam
As the song goes: "*Jaap Stam is a big Dutchman/Try a little trick and he'll make you look a prick*". Though his book trick might not have been his best idea.

11 v MANCHESTER CITY 1974

Stepney

Forsyth   Houston

Buchan   Holton

Morgan B. Greenhoff Martin Daly

Macari   McCalliog

27 April 1974
Old Trafford
Manchester United 0
Manchester City 1 (Law).
The King back-heels
and just six years after
conquering Europe,
United are relegated
to Division Two.

5. Ole Gunnar Solskjaer From the fjords with baby-faced love.

6. Andrei Kanchelskis
Faster than a Ukrainian election count.

7. Mikael Silvestre
Oh Mickey, you're so fine.

8. Cristiano Ronaldo
Sublime skills from Madeira. Though you wouldn't want his wardrobe advice.

9. Arnold Muhren
United director Maurice Watkins lists the Dutchman as his favourite ever Red.

10. Ronnie Johnsen
The Norwegian played in four successive trophy-winning matches..

11. Louis Saha
The Frenchman has taken up residence on the Johnsen memorial treatment table.

MANC LANDMARKS
Local places with United links

1. Eddie Colman Court, Salford
Ordsal boy Colman was a Busby Babe who perished at Munich. His name is dedicated to a tower block used as student accommodation by the University of Salford.

2. Davyhulme Park Golf Club
Before a gradual shift to the south of the city, Davyhulme was home to several United players in the 1950s and 1960s. The players met in Davyhulme's art deco clubhouse five miles west of Old Trafford for a pre-match steak.

3. Mottram Hall
Visiting European teams now usually stay at the Worsley Marriot rather than Mottram Hall, but the Cheshire hotel was where Fergie learned United were the champions of England in 1993 whilst having a round of golf. He joyfully informed a fellow golfer, a Japanese chap with Sharp (United's then sponsors) emblazoned on his jacket. The chap didn't have a clue what he was on about.

4. North Road, Newton Heath
United's first ground, between 1878 and 1893, was at North Road, now Northampton Road, in Newton Heath. The team changed half-a-mile away at the Three Crowns public house and the pitch was located on the edge of a clay pit. Today, the North Manchester Business Park lies where the pitch once stood. Previously, Moston Brook High School stood on the site and a plaque pointed out the site's significance. Until it was stolen.

5. Bank Street, Clayton
From 1893 to 1910, this was The Heathens' ground. Located amongst billowing factories, the setting was pure Lowry-scape. Today, the old pitch is a car park for the Manchester Velodrome, marked by a Red plaque on Bank Street. Manchester City's new stadium is but a Schmeichel kick away.

6. New Islington Hall, Ancoats
At a meeting in the New Islington Hall, Ancoats, in 1901, Harry Stafford, the club's full-back, made an offer to save Newton Heath from bankruptcy. Legend has it that a local brewer called John Davies stopped to admire Stafford's dog. Stafford explained the club's plight and Davies ended up buying the club, clearing its debt, suggesting a new red and white strip and a name. New Islington was an area of Ancoats that was wiped from the maps when a new estate, the notorious Cardroom, was built.

7. The Imperial Hotel
Not only was the PFA formed at a meeting in the Imperial Hotel, the name
Manchester United was decided there on 26 April 1902. Manchester Central and
Manchester Celtic were dismissed, the former because it sounded too much like
a railway station. Director Louis Rocca always claimed it was he who proposed
the name Manchester United. The hotel, close to Piccadilly Station, stood as
a public house until the 1990s before being demolished to make way for the
Malmaison Hotel.

8. Albert Square
Manchester is not noted for its open public spaces, but the town hall balcony
overlooking the square was the destination for many a victorious Red homecoming
parade. Safety concerns mean it's no longer used to show off new silverware. That
decision, 20 years ago, has yet to affect City.

9. George Best's old house, near Bramhall
Best referred to his newly commissioned house as his "Saturn Five space station
house". Fans besieged it in the early 1970s and played football on the lawn outside.
Architectural critics claimed it looked like a public lavatory. Inside, the lavish
furnishings consisted of the copious use of marble, full-length tinted windows...
and plenty of female visitors.

10. The Cliff, Lower Broughton, Salford
The Cliff was United's main training ground until the move to Carrington in 2000.
It's still in use as the main base for the Under-9s and Under-10s academy teams and,
until their recent demise, was home to the United Ladies team.

11. Lyttleton Road, Salford
Pre-Carrington, United's second training facility
was at Lyttleton Road, close to the Cliff and the old Manchester racecourse. The club
considered expanding this site before the move to the suburbs. Alex said of it: "It's
very exposed and the wind howls through the place. It could be a good training
ground but it would cost a lot of money."

MANCS, BORN AND BRED

"You from here and that?" Players born within spitting distance of Old Trafford

1. Brian Kidd and Nobby Stiles
Collyhurst lads who went to the same school. Stiles now lives in Stretford while Kidd has a house in Middleton, where he was frequently spotted training in a United tracksuit top. When he was assistant manager at Leeds.

2. Remi Moses
One of the few black kids to grow up in Miles Platting. A very hard player.

3. Phil Chisnall
The last player to transfer between United and Liverpool, over 40 years ago, is from Stretford. He now lives in Urmston and works in the malt-loaf factory.

4. Paul Scholes
The Langley Estate, near Middleton, where Ken Loach set his movie *Raining Stones*.

5. Shay Brennan
The 'Irishman' who made the goal that won the 1968 European Cup was born here.

6. Roger Byrne
The great captain of the Busby Babes was born in Gorton, died in Munich and is buried in Stretford.

7. Nicky Butt
Gorton's finest contemporary player.

8. Dennis Viollet
Prolific goalscorer who grew up in Moss Side and supported City as a kid.

9. Wes Brown
Longsight lad. As Manc as the Co-op Bank.

10. Eddie Colman and Geoff Bent
Both Salford. Both lost at Munich.

11. John Aston senior and junior
The father and son who played for United.

> SATURN FIVE SPACE STATION HOUSE, WAS HOW BEST REFERRED TO HIS NEW HOME

MEGASTORE MERCHANDISE [1]

11 best-selling items in the Old Trafford Megastore

1. Home shirts
2. Stationery (the three-pack of pens)
3. Car accessories
4. United chocolate bars
5. Club-crested keyrings
6. United cameras
7. Scarves
8. Hats
9. Player mugs
10. Plush toys
11. Footballs

MEGASTORE MERCHANDISE [2]

11 product ideas politely declined by the manager

1. United toilet roll
2. United condoms
3. United coffins
4. United toilet seats
5. United garters
6. United hub caps
7. United paving stones
8. United blow-up dolls
9. United cat flaps
10. United plasters
11. United edible knickers

NEARLY MEN

They could have been heroes, if only they had signed for United

1. Paul Gascoigne

The Newcastle youngster was a top priority for Fergie well before Gazza-mania.
A deal appeared to have been struck in 1989, but then Terry Venables moved in with
a superior financial offer to take the player to Spurs (something to do with buying
Gazza's parents a house). We can only speculate how the Geordie's career might
have panned out had he come under the watchful eye of the United manager.
But it is fair to suggest he would probably not now be living in Chris Evans's attic
and calling himself G8.

2. Ronaldinho

The dentally over-endowed Brazilian genius was as good as being measured for
a Red shirt in the summer of 2003. But Peter Kenyon (may his name be forever
cursed), charged with dotting the i's and crossing the t's on the deal, managed to
screw it up sufficiently so that a player who had publicly stated he wanted to move
to Manchester ended up in Barcelona. And look what he did for them. Regarded as
the biggest administrative disaster of the Ferguson era, Old Trafford insiders blame
only one man for the debacle.

3. Alan Shearer

Twice the Geordie bulldozer was meant to be coming to Old Trafford, and twice
wheelbarrow-loads of cash enticed Billy Moneybags elsewhere. When he was
leaving Blackburn Rovers, Shearer had even convinced Ferguson to gift him the
coveted No 9 shirt, and told the Boss he would like to take the penalties. Then he
took a phone call from Newcastle.

4. Peter Shilton

Tommy Docherty claims he would have won the league title in 1976 if Martin

Edwards and the board had agreed to his request to buy Peter Shilton – the then best goalkeeper in England. But they refused, Docherty played Paddy Roche instead, and immediately had enough material to keep him in after-dinner jokes for the rest of his days.

5. Arjen Robben
It is best not to utter the name Kenyon within earshot of Alex Ferguson. The best young Dutch player since Ruud van Nistelrooy had agreed terms with United to join them at the end of the 2004 season from PSV Eindhoven. His father – who is also his agent – several times spoke warmly of how Ferguson had monitored the boy's progress and how the family couldn't wait to work with him on a regular basis. But the United accountants screwed things up by trying to revise their offer – by a half. Miffed, PSV turned to Kenyon, who had arrived at Chelsea to help out with Roman Abramovich's cheque book. A big loss for United. Unlike…

6. Glen Hysen
Fergie was very keen to buy the prematurely-greying Swedish stopper from Fiorentina. Instead he opted to go to Anfield. Which, judging by the way he played at the heart of the Liverpool defence, was a lucky escape for United.

7. Charlie Nicholas
United wanted Celtic's champagne wideboy to join them in 1982. But then Arsenal intervened and the promise of the bright lights of London turned his head. No easy task, given the weight of his luxuriant mullet.

8. Kevin Mabbutt
Gary's older brother scored a hat-trick as Bristol City won 3-1 in a First Division game at Old Trafford in 1978. An already panicking Dave Sexton tried hard to lure Mabbutt north, but he decided to stay in Bristol because, believe it or not, the money was better there. Three years on, as Mabbutt drove his sports car around the town, City were plunging into the Fourth Division. And, driven by an unsustainable wage bill, heading towards bankruptcy.

9. Stuart Pearce
Psycho was an early target for Alex Ferguson when the boss arrived from Aberdeen. But Brian Clough, the player's manager at Nottingham Forest, refused to answer Fergie's phone calls. Once, when Fergie turned up at the City Ground with an offer, Cloughie instructed his secretary to tell the visitor he wasn't there, leaving the United boss in the car park for three hours. "What could I do?" Fergie said on his return. "Get an arrest warrant?"

10. Ferenc Puskas

The great Hungarian, the only man to score two hat-tricks in European Cup finals, found himself in exile in Italy in 1958 after defecting from the new pro-Soviet regime in his homeland. Banned by FIFA for 18 months, he was kicking his heels when, in the immediate aftermath of the Munich disaster, he was approached to see if he might come to Old Trafford to replace some of the fallen. He was thrilled, but FIFA would not relax the ban. Puskas stayed in Italy and eventually made his way to Real Madrid. Mind you, how long he would have stayed at Old Trafford when Madrid came calling is moot. United paid its players the FA maximum wage of £18 a week: when he signed for Madrid in August 1958, the Galloping Major was on £800.

11. Peter Beardsley

Beardsley was Fergie's first transfer objective when he arrived from Aberdeen, but Newcastle demanded £3m and United dropped out. Ferguson's mood was hardly improved when Beardsley joined Liverpool soon afterwards for £1.9m.

NICKNAMES

What did you just call me?

1. The Guvnor

Paul Ince's self-appointed nickname, which he put on his boots and his car. He'd also shout "Who's the guvnor?" during training but his team-mates still called him Incey.

2. PB (Popular Bill)

Sarcastic reference to Bill Foulkes's dressing-room popularity.

3. Blind Venetian

Possibly libellous moniker for keeper Massimo Taibi, who doesn't come from Venice.

4. Hayley

Was it just Victoria's revelation that Becks raided her wardrobe occasionally that reminded team-mates of the *Coronation Street* dimbo?

> ROY KEANE IS LIKENED TO THE OMEN'S DEVIL INCARNATE, DAMIEN – BY HIS TEAM-MATES

5. Choccy Brian McClair – as in eclair (geddit?).

6. The Bogota Bandit Charlie Mitten, much derided for taking the Colombian peso.

7. The Late Kevin Moran
After his tackle on Peter Reid in 1985: he was the first to be sent off in an FA Cup final.

8. Baby-faced Assassin
Ole Gunnar Solskjaer: a nickname that is still applicable in his fresh-faced thirties.

9. Old Brittle Bones
The injury-prone Jimmy Delaney.

10. Happy
Nobby Stiles, the man who moaned for Britain.

11. Damien
Roy Keane, likened unto *The Omen*'s Devil incarnate by his team-mates.

OLDEST REDS

I've come for me pension...

1. **46 years, 281 days** Billy Meredith, forward, 1921
2. **39 years, 48 days** Raimond van der Gouw, goalkeeper, 2002
3. **38 years, 240 days** Frank Mann, midfield, 1929
4. **38 years, 213 days** Jack Warner, midfield, 1950
5. **38 years, 5 days** Thomas Jones, defender, 1937
6. **37 years, 323 days** Teddy Partridge, forward, 1929
7. **37 years, 313 days** George Livingstone, forward, 1914
8. **37 years, 243 days** Clarence Hilditch, midfield, 1932
9. **37 years, 223 days** Bill Foulkes, defender, 1969
10. **37 years, 117 days** Bryan Robson, midfield, 1994
11. **37 years, 42 days** Jack Harding, midfield, 1935

ONLY A GAME

11 one-appearance wonders

1. Tony Hawksworth
A lance-corporal in the Tank Regiment, Hawksworth (who'd played for Sheffield United) received a call at work asking him to play in goal for United at Blackpool that afternoon in October 1956. United drew 2-2.

2. Harold Bratt
The Salford-born half-back played his only game for the Reds in front of United's lowest post-war crowd and finished on the losing side as Bradford City beat the Reds 2-1 in 1960's inaugural League Cup.

3. Dennis Walker
The first black player to wear United red. The Northwich-born forward came through the youth ranks and made his only senior appearance for United in a weakened pre-FA Cup final team away to Nottingham Forest in May 1963. United lost 3-2.

4. Jonathan Clark
The Swansea-born midfielder waited three years for his debut, against Sunderland at Old Trafford in October 1976. When it finally came, he gave the ball away with one of his first touches and the Mackems equalised.

5. 'Anto' Whelan
The Dubliner (signed from Bohemians for £30,000) came on as substitute for injured compatriot Kevin Moran in a home game against Southampton in 1980. The defender went back to Ireland to join Shamrock Rovers the following year.

6. Peter Beardsley
A £250,000 signing from Vancouver Whitecaps. The future Newcastle, Liverpool and England forward wore red for just 45 minutes in a 1982 League Cup tie against Bournemouth before being sold back again.

7. Colin McKee
A member of the 1992 FA Youth Cup-winning side, the Glaswegian winger played 75 minutes in the celebratory final game of the 1993/94 season, against Coventry.

8. Pat McGibbon
Not only was the defender's only game the 3-0 home defeat to York City in 1995, the Ulsterman also had the ignominy of being sent off.

9. Nick Culkin
The York-born goalkeeper boasts the shortest first-team career in United's history. The 6ft 3in, 21-year-old replaced Raimond van der Gouw for the final 80 seconds in a 2-1 victory at Arsenal in 1999.

10. Richard Wellens
The local midfielder was a Red for just 16 minutes in a 3-0 League Cup defeat to Aston Villa in 1999.

11. Jimmy Davis
The talented winger played in the 4-0 League Cup defeat at Arsenal in 2001, then spent two years out on loan. Tragically, he never got the opportunity to go further, being killed in a car accident on the M40 in 2003.

OOH AAH: 11 SONGS TO PLAYERS

Forlan? Wyn Davies? So great they got songs about them too...

1. Cantona
To the hymn tune...
What a friend we have in Jesus
He's our saviour from afar
What a friend we have in Jesus
And his name is… Cantona
Ooh aah Cantona

2. And the previous king…
To the Davy Crockett theme...
Son of a fisherman from Aberdeen
Played for his country when only 18
His football magic is a sight to see
As he leads United on to victory

(Chorus)
Denis, Denis Law
King of the Football League

3. John O'Shea
To the tune of *When Johnny Comes Marching Home*...

When Johnny goes marching down the wing
O'Shea, O'Shea
When Johnny goes marching down the wing
The Stretford End will always sing
We all know that Johnny will score a goal

4. Wyn Davies (towering early 1970s striker)
To the tune of Bob Dylan's *The Mighty Quinn*...
C'mon without
C'mon within
You ain't seen nothing
Like the mighty Wyn

5. Ole Gunnar Solskjaer
To the tune of *Skip to My Lou*...
Who put the ball in the Germans' net? (Ole, Ole)
Who put the ball in the Germans' net? (Ole, Ole)
Who put the ball in the Germans' net?
Ole Gunnar Solskjaer

6. Law, Best and Charlton
To the tune of The Beatles' *Ob-la-di, Ob-la-da*...
Bobby gets the ball on the centre spot
Passes it to Georgie on the wing
Georgie beats his man and puts in a cross for Denis Law
And it's a goal and he's the king
Ob-la-di, ob-la-da,
Man United, European champions

7. Diego Forlan
To the Italian lounge classic *Volare*...
Di-e-go, wo-oh
Di-e-go, wo-oh-oh
He came from Uruguay
He made the Scousers cry

8. Ian Rush
To the tune of *Rock The Boat* by The Hues Corporation...
Oh I'd like to know where
Rush got his nose from

9. Ryan Giggs
To the tune of Joy Division's *Love Will Tear Us Apart...*
Giggs,
Giggs will tear you apart…
Again

(There's also an ironic spin-off in honour of Old Trafford's finest step-over, by Neville, P:
"Phil, Phil will tear you apart…")

10. Brian Kidd
To the tune of The Beatles *Hello, Goodbye...*
Eusebio,
And I say Kiddo

11. Paul Scholes
Reds get biblical to the tune of *Kumbayaa...*
He scores goals galore
He scores goals
Paul Scholes he scores goals

OPPONENTS TO APPLAUD
Great performances for the wrong team

1. Dejan Savicevic Red Star Belgrade
The star player for the European champions Red Star Belgrade, Savicevic visited Manchester for the 1991 European Super Cup final. "Anyone at that game must still be wondering how we won it," said Ferguson. "I know I am. Savicevic was absolutely sensational."

2. Liam Brady Arsenal
The Gunners' Irish midfielder could certainly play, and never more so than when he came to Old Trafford. Was he hoping to be noticed?

3. Eric Cantona Leeds United
It's not often that K-Stand applauds a visiting player, but the spontaneity which greeted an overhead kick by the then Leeds United forward in September 1992 was recognition of genius. Steve Bruce and Gary Pallister rushed to tell their manager the same. Two months later Cantona crossed the Pennines.

4. Stefan Effenberg Bayern Munich
Bayern's main man, Effenberg outclassed Keane in his prime as the vengeful German team beat United home and away in the 2001 Champions League.

5. Marco van Basten AC Milan
Although he only appeared at Old Trafford in a 1988 friendly, the Dutch striker was the star at a time when Milan were football's Harlem Globetrotters and United averaged 38,000 crowds. They had Franco Baresi, we had Colin Gibson; they had Ruud Gullit, we had Liam O'Brien; they had Frank Rijkaard, we had Graeme Hogg. You get the picture.

6 . Ronaldo Real Madrid
The gifted Brazilian scored a hat-trick in Real Madrid's 4–3 defeat at Old Trafford in April 2003. He was applauded off the field when substituted and said he felt "honoured by appreciation of the Manchester fans."

7. Dennis Bailey QPR
An oddity, but like Ronaldo, the Fulham reject scored a hat-trick at Old Trafford, on New Year's Day 1992. Ronaldo subsequently fared rather better; Bailey managed just one more league goal for QPR before trailing through the lower divisions.

8. Edgar Davids and Zinedine Zidane Juventus
Juventus's 1999 midfield pairing completely dominated the first leg of the European Cup semi-final at Old Trafford in 1999. A late Ryan Giggs goal gave United a draw they hardly deserved.

9. Bryan Robson West Bromwich Albion
West Brom's Laurie Cunningham was the speedy star, Cyril Regis its dynamic focal point, yet a young Robson – complete with bubble perm – bulldozed the Baggies to a 5-3 win at Old Trafford in December 1978.

10. Fernando Redondo Real Madrid
"Redondo's forward run and beautiful turn past Henning Berg was football of the highest class." That's what Roy Keane reckoned of Madrid's best player, the man who stopped United retaining the European Cup in 2000.

11. Robbie Fowler
Perhaps not.

> RONALDO SAID HE FELT "HONOURED BY THE APPRECIATION OF THE MANCHESTER FANS" AFTER HIS HAT-TRICK

OWN GOALS

And you don't even need to be on the pitch to score them

1. Becoming a PLC 1991
Since Martin Edwards floated United on the stock exchange in order to raise money to redevelop the Stretford End, more than 20 times as much has been paid out in dividends as was put into the club by those original investors. Not that Edwards minded, he was a chief beneficiary, trousering a good few million in divvies himself. Ultimately, having shares available on the open market paved the way for the hostile takeover by Malcolm Glazer.

2. Lee Martin v Montpellier, Cup Winners' Cup March 1991
The defender had been the hero of the previous year's 1-0 FA Cup victory over Crystal Palace, scoring the goal that allowed United to compete in Europe. He now went from hero to zero by scoring for the French team in the first leg of the quarter-final and was substituted. The game ended 1-1 but United won the away leg 2-0 and went on to lift the trophy. Poor Martin wasn't so fortunate. Having injured his back, he missed out on beating Barcelona and subsequently lost his place when Paul Parker and Denis Irwin arrived next season.

3. The grey kit
Fergie blamed a 3-1 defeat away against Southampton in April 1996 on the famous grey kit (the players, he said, couldn't pick one another out against the crowd, and they changed at half-time). The rest of the world knew the turgid confection, with its panel of red vertical stripes, was a sartorial disaster from the start.

4. Changing the badge July 1998
According to official sources, the words "football" and "club" were removed from the United crest in order to "simplify the brand image". Why not just turn it into a £ sign and have done with it?

5. The board recommends the Murdoch takeover September 1999
The fans just don't listen and campaign against the BSkyB bid for all they are worth. They win.

6. Not defending the FA Cup 2000
Officially this was to allow United, as European Cup holders, to take part in the first World Club Championships in Brazil. But there were dark mutterings of government pressure being put on the club not to upset FIFA by declining to participate, thus supposedly endangering England's bid for the 2006 World Cup. Fergie's face at the

press conference – which announced the club's withdrawal from the world's oldest football competition in order to compete in the world's most pointless – said it all.

7. Roy Keane v Real Madrid, Champions League March 2000
Desperate to play in the Champions League final after missing out the year before, Roy arrives at the far post with perfect timing to ram the ball home at Old Trafford. Heart-breakingly, it was at the wrong end.

8. Wes Brown v Valencia, Champions League March 2001
A spectacular diving header by Wesley gifts the Spaniards an equaliser at Old Trafford. The point allows Valencia to top the second stage group and they eventually reach the final, losing to Real.

9. Forgetful Rio Ferdinand misses a drugs test January 2004
He is out shopping, Rio says, having forgotten to take a routine drugs test after training. But the defence does nothing for him and he is banned for nine months by the FA, during which Arsenal win the league. Not much point forking out £30m for the best centre-back in Britain for him to sit in the stands.

10. What colour do we play in again?
From 1993 onwards, to promote shirt sales, United's marketing department change the strip repeatedly. In five seasons between 2000 and 2005 United play at Highbury in shirts of five different hues. Cue the usual rip-off stories in the papers.

11. Richard Dunne February 2005
Playing for City, the well-upholstered Irishman slices horribly into his own net from a Wayne Rooney cross. Just goes to show there are some own goals you never get tired of watching.

THE WORDS 'FOOTBALL' AND 'CLUB' ARE REMOVED FROM THE CREST. WHY NOT JUST TURN IT INTO A £ SIGN?

PARTNERSHIPS

Twos and threes we've immortalised

1. Law, Best and Charlton
Busby's holy trinity, the most famous forward line in English football, bestrode the world for six years.

2. Bruce and Pallister
Dolly and Daisy they called themselves. Provided the foundation on which the 1990s glories were forged.

3. The Greenhoff brothers
Brian came through the youth ranks, Jimmy arrived from Stoke City. Together they enjoyed the best of The Doc's Red era.

4. The Neville brothers
Gary and Phil, loved by Reds, loathed by everyone else. Together they redefine the term shirty Mancs.

5. Rooney and Ronaldo
Cristiano, that is. The same age and on the same wavelength: the best two teenagers in world football.

6. McGrath and Whiteside
The team within United's legendary 1980s drinking team. The last straw for Fergie was when the pair appeared together, plastered, on Granada's *Kick Off* show the night before an FA Cup match against QPR in 1989. They were soon on the way out.

7. Coppell and Hill
Tommy Doc's flying wingers weren't exactly soul mates. Coppell, studious and

purposeful, Hill mercurial and flighty. "People made comparisons," Coppell remembers, nearly 30 years on, "but our personalities reflected the way we played, his highs were higher, his lows lower."

8. Keane and Scholes
"Is there any better midfield pairing in Europe?" John Motson asked during the 2005 season. The answer is no. Sir Alex's toughest managerial challenge will be replacing them.

9. Cole and Yorke
For two seasons they were electric, and central to the Treble. But then Dwight's appetites got the better of him, and both ended up at Blackburn Rovers.

10. The McShanes
Harry played on the wing in the early 1950s (and was Old Trafford's PA announcer in the early 1970s). His son, Paul, is United-mad Ian, who would happily have swapped all the adulation and cash from starring in *Lovejoy* and *Deadwood* for the chance to slip on a United shirt.

11. The Fergusons
Sir Alex and son Darren are the only father/son, manager/player combination in United history.

POP STARS AND OTHER FAIRWEATHER FANS

"Just one of those teams that you see now and then?" Here are 11 not-so-frequent visitors to Old Trafford who like to profess allegiance

1. Mick Hucknall
The ginger soul singer was allowed to train with United before the 4–0 defeat to Barcelona in 1994, leading one player (now who could that have been?) to say: "Is this a f**king circus?"

2. Ian Brown
Art imitates life. The ex-Stone Roses frontman imitates his idol, George Best.

3. Zoe Ball
She's got a portrait of Eric Cantona in her Brighton front room.

4. Simon Le Bon
The Duran Duran singer struggled to get in to the post-match players' party in Barcelona, 1999. Having model wife Yasmin on his arm probably swung it for him.

5. Ulrika Johnsson
She used a game at Old Trafford to practise her Swedish on Sven-Goran Eriksson.

6. Bertie Ahern
The Irish Taoiseach is a Red.

7. Martin McGuinness
And so is Sinn Fein's deputy leader.

8. Morrissey
Urmston-born, Stretford-bred, the Smiths' singer was a Red, once losing his scarf at a game. Is he now? He probably doesn't know himself.

9. Davy Jones
The former Monkee from Manchester. Now living in LA.

10. Tim Burgess
Another LA-based Red. Brian McClair is a big fan of this Charlatan.

11. Peter Noone
Herman's Hermits' front man, who sold 50 million records. Guess which US state starting 'Ca' he lives in?

PUBS
Where you'll find the odd Red shirt

1. The Trafford
Situated at the top of Sir Matt Busby Way, it's the closest pub to Old Trafford. Normally the first stop for news crews to get a Red fan opinion from someone with a Manchester accent.

2. The Bishop's Blaze
Want to sing songs about City, Scousers and Leeds on a loop? In conditions similar to a Turkish steam bath? Join the queue outside. On the Chester Road in Stretford.

3. The Quadrant
Close to the Lancashire Cricket ground in In Stretford, this was a favoured hangout of the Busby Babes, many of whom had lodgings nearby. Tommy Taylor had an understanding with the publican who would quietly refill his glass under the counter with gin while he had a bottle of tonic on the table.

4. The Peveril of the Peak
Eric Cantona was known to call into this wonderful Victorian pub for a pint and a game of table football. Against the well-practised regulars, he didn't quite make the impact that he made on a real pitch. On Great Bridgewater Street in Castlefield.

5. Best's hangouts
In the 1960s and 1970s Best drank in the Brown Bull pub near Salford Crescent, and in Blinkers, an intimate basement club with coved seating on Bridge Street. Anabelle's on Brazenoze Street was another favoured Best haunt, and he later became a partner in the Slack Alice club. All have since closed or changed names.

6. The Gorse Hill
Big Victorian pub on the A56 in Stretford. Popular with supporters' clubs branches on match days.

7. Sam Platts
Modern pub overlooking the Manchester Ship canal and Salford Quays. Where the Independent Manchester United Supporters Association and some of Shareholders United's 20,000 members meet before games.

8. The Tollgate
Modern pub opposite Trafford Bar Metro Station. Always busy pre-match with Reds.

9. The White Lion, Castlefield
United memorabilia adorns the wall of this boozer on Liverpool Road. The Red landlord also organises barges to home games from outside. Try it.

10. The Living Room
The discreet top floor of this Deansgate bar is where several United players like to chill. Although it's so dark you wonder how they can see each other.

11. Sugar Lounge
Pretentious bar that's popular with celebrities (as in 18-year-old *Coronation Street* actors) and a regular footballer hangout.

PUNDITS

"Just fill for 30, love..." Pundits that were all former Reds

1. Garth Crooks King of the 20-clause question, BBC
2. Pat Crerand Red-eyed at MUTV
3. Gary Pallister Keeps Ray Stubbs company on BBC's *Final Score*
4. Alan Brazil Mr Foot in Mouth himself on *talkSPORT*
5. Gordon Strachan Sassenachs struggle to understand a word he utters on the *Match Of The Day 2* sofa. Their loss
6. Gary Bailey South Africa's Des Lynam, minus the 'tache
7. Mickey Thomas Entirely hair-free on Century FM
8. George Best Regular in those strange, one-speaker headphones on Sky's Gillette *Soccer Saturday*.
9. Ray Wilkins Programmed never to say anything negative about anyone on Sky
10. Eamon Dunphy Roy Keane's ghost and now Ireland's premier controversialist
11. Ron Atkinson Available for work anytime, any place these days…

QUOTE, UNQUOTE (1): ALEX FERGUSON

"And you can quote me on that." Here's a selection of choice cuts from Fergie

1. "You get one of these once in a lifetime and I got mine at Maine Road."
After the 5-1 defeat to City, November 1989

2. "I have never done anything like it before, and I don't want to do anything like it again, ever. He was absolutely sick, sick to his boots. Poor old Jim, he hasn't got a rhino hide."
On dropping Jim Leighton for the FA Cup final replay, May 1990

3. "Get rid of the lot of them. You're back in digs."
To the host, on turning up unannounced at a party at Lee Sharpe's house, April 1992.

4. "Remember this day and just how important you are at Manchester United. What has just happened should tell you all how much people envy you. They wouldn't have done that otherwise. It proves how big we are."
To Lee Sharpe, Ryan Giggs and Paul Ince after Liverpool fans had asked for their autographs, then ripped the paper up and thrown it in their faces, April 1992

5. "Of all the many qualities a good team must possess, the supreme essential for me is penetration. And Eric brought the can-opener."
Assessing Cantona, May 1993

6. "When the Italians tell you it's pasta on the plate, I check under the sauce to make sure it really is."
Doubting the integrity of his hosts before the Champions League quarter-final against Internazionale in March 1999

7. "Football: bloody hell."
Repeatedly, the night of the Champions League victory, May 1999

8. "Can't I have two?"
When asked at a 2003 charity dinner which he would shoot first – Posh or Wenger – if he had a gun and only one bullet

9. "It was just one of those things that happen in football."
After the affair of the flying boot and Beckham's eyebrow, February 2003

10. "What 19-year-old has maturity? Jesus Christ, at 19 I was trying to start a workers' revolution in Glasgow. My mother thought I was a communist. She was down on her knees praying every night."
On Wayne Rooney, after the boy wonder's little tantrum in Madrid while playing for England against Spain, November 2004

11. "There's no wimps in my team."
After the demolition of Arsenal at Highbury, February 2005

"YOU GET ONE OF THESE ONCE IN A LIFETIME AND I GOT MINE AT MAINE ROAD."

QUOTE, UNQUOTE (2): ERIC

Nobody in football gives quotes like Eric. José Mourinho? Big Ron? You're not even on the same pitch, guys...

1. "When seagulls follow the trawler they are hoping for sardines to be thrown into the sea."

2. "I imagine the ball to be alive, sensitive, responding to the touch of my foot, to my caresses, like a woman with the man she loves."

3. "In the modern game of football there are great musicians, but Glenn Hoddle is like Mozart among the hard rock men."

4. "An artist, in my eyes, is someone who can lighten up a dark room. I have never, and never will, find any difference between the pass from Pelé to Carlos Alberto in the final of the World Cup in 1970 and the poetry of young Rimbaud. There is, in each of these human manifestations, an expression of beauty which touches us and gives us a feeling of eternity."

5. "I leave when I need to change. It's like being with a woman. If you get to the point when you've got nothing left to say to her, you leave. Or else you stop being good."

6. "I only know one way to take penalties – to score them."

7. "In England everything is beautiful. The stadiums are beautiful, the atmosphere is beautiful, the cops on horseback are beautiful. The crowds respect you."

8. "I value truth, honesty, respect for one another, compassion and understanding. I have found these qualities in Manchester United."

9. "I've been punished for striking a goalkeeper. For spitting at supporters. For throwing my shirt at a referee. For calling my manager a bag of shit. I called those who judged a bunch of idiots. I thought I might have trouble finding a sponsor."

10. "And I want to apologise to the prostitute I shared my bed with last evening." Eric prostrates himself before the FA

11. "I have played professional football for 13 years, which is a long time. I now wish to do other things. I have always planned to retire at the top, and at Manchester United I have reached the pinnacle of my career."

QUOTE, UNQUOTE (3): THE BEST OF THE REST

Anything you'd like to say to the press, then?

1. "99 per cent of footballers will tell you they want to play for Manchester United. And the other one per cent are liars."
Gordon McQueen on moving from the Reds' feeder club, Leeds United, 1979

2. "It's like Vietnam out there."
Big Ron, a tad hyperbolic after he was tear-gassed by home fans when he arrived for a game at Anfield, 1985

3. "I used to drive home from Manchester United training along the M56 and there was a left turn for Wilmslow, where I lived, and a right turn for Hale, where Norman Whiteside, Paul McGrath and Bryan Robson lived. I used to say that it was left for under three pints a night and right for more than ten."
Gordon Strachan on his time at Old Trafford, 1986

4. "When the TV people asked me if I wanted to play a football manager in a drama I asked how long it would take. 'About ten days,' they said. 'Aye,' I said, 'that's about par for the course.'"**Tommy Docherty**, 1994

5. "I just yelled: 'Off you go Cantona, it's an early shower for you.'"
Matthew Simmons explains precisely what it was he said to provoke Eric's attack on him at Selhurst Park in 1995

6. "A right pair of busy c**ts."
Jaap Stam on the Neville brothers, 2000

7. "Nobody tells me what to wear to a wedding."
Roy Keane reacts to an invite to the Posh/Becks nuptials, complete with instructions to don purple, 2000

8. "We've got so many wider interests…fashion, make-up. I mean, you think, football's great. But you've got to look at the wider picture."
Victoria Beckham, 2002

9. "The ball was there to be won (I think). I'd waited long enough. I hit him hard: take that you c**t. And don't ever stand over me again sneering about fake injuries."
Roy Keane after scything Manchester City's Alf Inge Haaland, 2002

10. "That's what children do – throw food. That's not fighting. We were real men. We'd have chinned them."
George Best on the Battle of the Buffet at Old Trafford, October 2004

11. "I'll see you out there."
Roy Keane to Patrick Vieira, in the tunnel, Highbury, February 2005

RED, WHITE AND GREY: 11 KITS TO REMEMBER

Or in the case of the vanishing grey shirts, to forget...

1. 1961-69 Plain red, with a round, white, vicar-style collar
Cool, simple, never bettered.

2. 1974/75 Plain scarlet, with a white, polo-style button-up collar
The team slip into the Second Division but comfort for Red fashion-junkies comes from a superbly designed home top. Class.

3. 1978-80 Adidas's first Red effort
Neat, sharp, unfussy. The opposite of the football Dave Sexton made his lads play.

4. 1994/95 The black change strip
Umbro's best in their tenure as United shirtmakers. Eric looks magnificent in it as, collar up, he leaps over the Selhurst Park barriers.

5. 1958 Short red sleeve
The last-ever photograph of the Busby Babes sees the lads lining up in a Belgrade freeze-out in short sleeves, v-necks and not a pair of gloves in sight.

6. 1990-92 Sixties Retro
Adidas's final home shirt pays homage to the 1960s United look. A bit too busy

11. v RED STAR BELGRADE 1958

Gregg

Byrne   Colman

Edwards   Foulkes   Jones

Charlton   Viollet   Taylor   Scanlon   Morgans

5 February 1958
European Cup, quarter-final,
second leg,
Belgrade.
Manchester United 3
(Charlton 2, Viollet)
Red Star 3 (Kostic 2, Tasic).
The last game the Busby
Babes ever played, 24 hours
before Munich.

round the collar to qualify as a classic, but miles better than what is to come.

7. 1993/94 Yellow and green halves, with a lace-up collar
Umbro's effort to celebrate the United centenary is apparently styled on Newton Heath's original colours. Naff is a kind word.

8. 1991/92 Blue flecks Madchester away
Adidas's blue-flecked acid nightmare snow-storm away shirt is meant to be a nod to Madchester style. Looks as silly on the pitch as it does with baggy jeans.

9. 1992/93 Red lace
Umbro's first home look is horrible: pointless lace-up detail and ugly graphics.

10. 1992/93 Blue and black
The away number is even worse: royal blue, covered with black doodlings that make it look as though it has been designed by a gorilla attempting *The Times* crossword.

11. 1995/96 Grey is not the colour
Umbro's grey third-change shirt provided enough material for a style disaster movie.

SEASONS TO FORGET

It hasn't always been glory, glory Man Utd…

1. 1921/22: Bottom of the table

Up until World War 2, United were not considered the colossus they are today. The club spent 12 consecutive seasons in Division Two on either side of the turn of the previous century and, apart from the Ernest Mangall-led purple patch between 1908 and 1911, didn't lay any claims to domestic dominance. The 1920s were an especially bad time for United, despite some huge crowds – including the current club home record of 70,504, against Aston Villa in 1920. 1922 was about as poor as it got – the Reds finished bottom of the First Division, winning just eight league games, and were watched by crowds as low as 9,000. The manager, John Robson, didn't hang around. He resigned at the start of the season and was replaced by John Chapman – who was later sacked after the FA ordered his suspension for alleged improper conduct.

2. 1933/34: Down with the Leeds

The Great Depression, which bit deep into Manchester's industrial wealth, was reflected in United's performances in the 1930s. They went down with Leeds United in 1931, finishing bottom after losing their first 12 games of the season – a Football League record – and winning just seven games all year. Not only that, but they conceded 115 goals and were walloped 7-4 by Newcastle United, 7-0 by Aston Villa and saw three other teams put six past them. United were £30,000 in debt and would surely have gone under, had the club not been saved by the money of businessman James Gibson. On the pitch, United came within a game of being relegated to the Third Division – the club's all-time nadir. They had to endure a trip to 20th-placed Millwall on the final day of the season, when the London side needed only a draw to stay up and send United down. In the event, the Reds rallied and won 2-0.

3. 1936/37: United down, City are champions

United went down and City won the league; how's that for a season? There was another dramatic finale – and this one went against United. Facing relegation, United lost their final game of the season to sit level on points with Leeds – who had a game still to play. For United to stay up, Portsmouth had to beat Leeds 2-0 at Elland Road, but Leeds won 3-1 and United went down. Manager Scott Duncan didn't stay around to see out his five-year contract, resigning to join non-league Ipswich. It meant that club secretary Walter Crickmer filled in until United's next manager was appointed after World War 2, one Matt Busby.

4. 1961/62: United lose the plot

English football changed forever in 1962 with the abolition of the maximum wage. In theory, a big club like United should have prospered, given that they could afford to pay higher wages than the majority. In reality, United offered players £25 a week plus £5 appearance money when Second Division teams like Sunderland were offering twice that. The glory of the Busby Babes was long forgotten as United went ten games without a win in the autumn, and when United needed new talent and inspiration, just three players – Phil Chisnall, Sammy McMillan and David Herd – debuted. The gloom was compounded by striker Dennis Viollet, he of 178 United goals, departing suddenly for Stoke City. He was said to be too fond of Manchester's nightlife. United were a shambles and nobody knew which direction the club was heading. Manager Matt Busby had to think hard about the club's future.

5. 1962/63: Still losing

Matt Busby switched his attacking Denis's. Out went Viollet and in came Law for a British record fee of £115,000 from Torino. The fee placed United in debt for the first time since the war. It was Busby's biggest gamble, but Law's initial success (he scored seven minutes into his debut and 23 goals in his first season) couldn't stop United's league form deteriorating. Another costly signing, Pat Crerand, bought from Celtic, entered a divided changing room. Bobby Charlton was being played out of position on the wing and various cliques blamed each other for United's poor form. Busby called a meeting to clear the air and trainer Jack Crompton was, somewhat unfairly, cited as the main problem by some players. There were also financial tensions, with United the lowest payers in the First Division. And an atrocious winter meant United didn't play between Boxing Day and 23rd February. United lost 20 of the 42 league games and finished in 19th position, only avoiding relegation by three points. They did win the FA Cup, though.

> IN 1962 MATT BUSBY TOOK HIS BIGGEST GAMBLE BUYING DENIS LAW FOR £115,000

6. 1972/73: The Ted McDougall months

United's slide began almost as soon as the club won the European Cup in 1968.
In succession, United finished 11th, eighth, eighth and, in 1972/73, 18th. By that time
the team was an ageing and transitional one which failed to win until the tenth
league game of the season. No fewer than 11 players had their last games for United
in 1972/73, including the two main talents of the previous decade, Bobby Charlton
and Denis Law. Another, George Best, was at his most troublesome due to his
extra-curricular excesses and his contract was terminated by "mutual agreement".
Stuck at the foot of the First Division, the cheque book was produced to buy Ted
McDougall from Bournemouth for £200,000 and Wyn Davies from City for £65,000.
Neither could arrest the poor form and neither lasted more than a few months at
a troubled Old Trafford. Following a 5-0 thrashing away at Crystal Palace in
December, genial manager Frank O'Farrell was dismissed. Scotland manager Tommy
Docherty took over, lavishing more money and making drastic changes. He would
bring six Scottish players: George Graham, Alex Forsyth, Lou Macari, Jim Holton,
Stewart Houston and Jim McCalliog as well as others. The new players breathed life
into the club and a spring revival saw United avoid relegation by finishing 18th.
There was little salvation in the Cups either. Wolves knocked United out of the FA
Cup in the third round and Bristol Rovers did likewise in the League cup, winning
2-1...at Old Trafford.

7. 1973/74: Relegation

Any optimism derived from the new-look United soon evaporated with a finish
in 21st place and the club's first relegation in 37 years. The defence was secure,
conceding just 48 goals – the best since winning the league in 1967 – but up front
United endured the bleakest goalscoring run in their history, scoring just 25 times
in the first 33 games. At one point, the leading scorer was goalkeeper Alex Stepney!
(He took the penalties.) George Best was tempted out of retirement to help the
cause mid-season, but the plot failed and he finally quit for good after 12 games.
A six-match unbeaten run towards the end of the season gave United a
mathematical chance of staying up – an opportunity which hinged on many
imponderables. It was vital that United beat City going into the last Saturday of the
season – a defeat would put United down. With eight minutes remaining and the
score at 0-0, City striker Denis Law back-heeled the ball past Alex Stepney to seal
United's fate. It was his last touch in club football and United were down.

8. 1980/81: The Garry Birtles years

It was the bleakest season since the relegation year in 1973. Under Dave Sexton,
United suffered humiliating defeats in the early rounds of both the FA and League
Cups. In the UEFA Cup, a team few had heard of, Polish side Widzew Lodz, knocked

United out. It got worse. Sexton's side managed just eight league wins in their first 35 games and at one stage didn't score a single goal in five consecutive matches – a club record. Two players made their United debuts during the 1980/81. One, Mike Duxbury, cost nothing. The other, striker Garry Birtles, cost a club record £1.25m as a replacement for Milan-bound Joe Jordan. Neither made their mark. Average gates were 6,500 down on the previous season and the directors, led by new chairman Martin Edwards, could take no more – Sexton was sacked less than a week after the final game of the season. Three managers – Ron Saunders, Lawrie McMenemy and Bobby Robson – all turned down the United job before the club's fourth choice, Ron Atkinson, took up the challenge.

9. 1988/89: Rubbish football, poor support

Alex Ferguson had had two years' experience in the United job and there was significant optimism about his progress after a second place finish in 1987/88. Mark Hughes returned from Barcelona and a young Lee Sharpe signed from Torquay. Mal Donaghy, Jim Leighton and Ralph Milne arrived too. Unfortunately, the optimism proved misguided as United registered just three wins in the first 14 league games. The Hughes-McClair partnership delivered only 24 goals – although McClair had a legitimate headed goal disallowed in the FA Cup sixth round at home to Nottingham Forest. Out of both cups, United slipped to 11th by the end of the season and, disillusioned with the football on offer, gates dropped too – just 23,368 saw Wimbledon's visit. That meant Liverpool overtook United as best-supported team, little surprise when United's record for the final 11 games read: W2 D 2 L7. It wasn't good enough…

10. 1989/90: Fergie must go

A 13th-place finish is not acceptable for a club of United's stature. It wouldn't be now and it wasn't then. Expensive new signings like Danny Wallace, Paul Ince, Gary Pallister, Mike Phelan and Neil Webb arrived and naturally enough, took time to gel. Yet United fans were growing restless after a succession of below-par seasons. "Fergie Out" banners appeared and fanzines prospered amidst the discontent. This was the season of the humiliating 5-1 derby defeat and a winless league run that stretched from 18 November to 10 February. The papers were convinced that Alex Ferguson was about to be dismissed, but the club stuck by its manager, recognising that he was getting things together behind the scenes, with Sir Bobby Charlton in particular arguing that fortunes would improve. On the bright side, United's FA Cup final victory was achieved without a game being played at Old Trafford – evidence of an emerging team spirit. If only there had been more of it in the league.

11. 1994/95: You don't win things without Eric...
United were second at the start of 1995, one point behind a wily Blackburn Rovers and their prolific goalscorer Alan Shearer. Old Trafford's top scorer at the turn of the year was not even a forward, but Andrei Kanchelskis – hence the move for Andy Cole in January 1995. Cole's signing was visionary, for Eric Cantona would play no further part in the season following a low-profile indiscretion at Selhurst Park. But this was not to be his glory season. Although United beat Blackburn home and away and never gave up chasing, the league went right to the wire, with United needing to beat West Ham United away on the final day to claim the championship. Mark Hughes and Andy Cole had clear chances, but once again Red dreams came unstuck at Upton Park. Bad went to worse, as United finished the season without so much as a trophy, after an FA Cup final defeat by Everton.

SHOCKERS...

The worst-ever defeats

1. **0–7** v Blackburn Rovers (a) Division One, April 1926
2. **0–7** v Aston Villa (a) Division One, December 1930
3. **0–7** v Wolves (a) Division Two, December 1931
4. **0–6** v Leicester City (a) Division One, March 1961
    0–6 v Ipswich Town (a) Division One, March 1980
    0–6 v Aston Villa (h) Division One, March 1914
    0–6 v Huddersfield Town (h) Division One, September 1930
8. **1–7** v Burnley (a) FA Cup, February 1901
    1–7 v Newcastle United (h) Division One, September 1927
10. **2–7** v Sheffield Wednesday (h) FA Cup, February 1961
11. **0–5** v Manchester City (h) Division One, February 1955

SHORTEST REDS

Does your mother know you're out?

1   **5ft 4in Terry Gibson** forward (1985-1987)
    5ft 4in Ernest Taylor forward (1957-1959)
    5ft 4in Billy Wrigglesworth forward (1936-1947)
4. **5ft 5in Danny Wallace** forward (1989-1993)
    5ft 5in Herbert Burgess defender (1906-1910)

5ft 5in Henry Cockburn midfielder (1946-1954)
7. **5ft 5 1/2in Gordon Strachan** midfielder (1984-1989)
8. **5ft 6in Steve Coppell** forward (1975-1983)
   5ft 6in John Fitzpatrick defender (1964-1973)
   5ft 6in Jesper Olsen forward (1984-1989)
   5ft 6in Nobby Stiles midfielder (1960-1971)
   5ft 6in Johnny Giles midfielder (1959-1963)

SO ****ING EASY

11 highest-scoring United victories

1. **10-0** v Anderlecht (Maine Road) European Cup, September 1956
2. **10-1** v Wolves (h) Division One, October 1892
3. **9-0** v Ipswich (h) Premiership, March 1995
   9-0 v Walsall Town Swifts (h) Division Two, April 1895
   9-0 v Darwen (h) Division Two, December 1898
6. **8-0** Yeovil Town (h) FA Cup, February 1949
7. **8-1** Nottingham Forest (a) Premiership, February 1999
8. **8-2** Northampton Town (a) FA Cup, January 1970
9. **7-0** Grimsby Town (a) Division Two, December 1899
10. **7-1** Chesterfield (a) Division Two, November 1937
    7-1 Brentford (h) FA Cup, January 1928

SONGS TO REMEMBER

The top Red classics

1. Manchester United Calypso

(composed by Edric Connor, early 1960s)
Oh Manchester, Manchester United
A bunch of bouncing Busby Babes
They deserve to be knighted
Whenever they're playing in your town
Be sure to get to that football ground
Take a lesson, come and see
The football taught by Matt Busby
Oh, Manchester, Manchester United

A bunch of bouncing Busby babes
they deserve to be knighted.

2. Forever And Ever
(To the tune of *Forever And Ever*)
Forever and ever
We'll follow the boys
Of Manchester United
The Busby Babes.

3. I See The Stretford End Arising
(To Creedence Clearwater Revival's *Bad Moon Rising*)
I see the Stretford End arising
I see the trouble on the way
Don't go out tonight
If you don't wear Red and white
'Cos I've seen the Stretford Enders fight.

4 The Banks Of The River Irwell
(To the Sousa march)
From the banks of the River Irwell, to the shores of Sicily
We will fight, fight, fight for United, 'til we win the Football League
To hell with Liverpool, to hell with Man City (they're shit!)
We will fight, fight, fight for United, 'til we win the Football League.

5. The Stretford Enders
(To a nice Cockerney lilt)
Bertie Mee said to Matt Busby
"Have you heard of the North Bank, Highbury?"
"No," said Matt, "you Cockney twat
But I've heard of the Stretford Enders."

6. Hello, Hello
(To the tune of *Follow Follow*)
Hello! Hello! We are the Busby boys!
Hello! Hello! We are the Busby boys!
And if you are a City fan surrender or you'll die
We all follow United!

7. The Pride Of All Europe
(Terrace tune)
We are just one of those teams that you see now and then
We often score six but we seldom score ten
We beat 'em at home and we beat 'em away
We kill any bastards that get in our way.
We are the pride of all Europe, the cock of the north
We hate the Scousers, the cockneys of course (and Leeds)
We are United without any doubt, we are the Manchester boys

Na, na na, na, na, na, na, na, na, na, na, na...

8. What Do You Want To Go To Wembley for?
(Terrace tune)
What do you want to go to Wembley for?
Take a trip down Oldham Road, and you're in Ireland
Take a walk down Ancoats Lane, and you're in Italy grand
China and Japan in Upper Brook Street
Greengate and you're in Alabam
And if you keep walking still
Palestine's in Cheetham Hill
So what do you wanna go to Wembley for?
To see United!

9. Glory Glory Man United
(To the tune of Glory! Glory! Hallelujah)
Glory, glory Man United,
Glory, glory Man United,
Glory, glory Man United
And the Reds go marching on, on, on!

I SEE THE STRETFORD END ARISING
I SEE THE TROUBLE ON THE WAY

10. By Far The Greatest Team
(to the tune of The Wild Rover)
And it's Man United
Man United FC
We're by far the greatest team
The world has ever seen!

11. The Flowers Of Manchester

(Terrace tune)

One cold and bitter Thursday, in Munich, Germany
Eight great football stalwarts conceded victory
Eight men will never play again, who met destruction there
The flowers of English football, the flowers of Manchester
Matt Busby's boys were flying, returning from Belgrade
This great United family, all masters of their trade
The pilot of the aircraft, the skipper captain Thain
Three times they tried to take off and twice turned back again
The third time down the runway disaster followed close
There was slush upon that runway and the aircraft never rose
It ploughed into the marshy ground, it broke, it overturned
And eight of that team were killed when the blazing wreckage burned.

Roger Byrne and Tommy Taylor who were capped for England's side
And Ireland's Billy Whelan and England's Geoff Bent died
Mark Jones and Eddie Colman and David Pegg also
They all lost their lives as it ploughed on through the snow
Big Duncan went too, with an injury to his brain
And Ireland's brave Jack Blanchflower will never play again
The great Matt Busby lay there, the father of this team
Three long months passed by before he saw his team again
The trainer, coach and secretary and a member of the crew
Eight great sporting journalists who with United flew
And one of them was Big Swifty who we will ne'er forget
The finest English keeper, that ever graced a net.

> "THE FLOWERS OF ENGLISH FOOTBALL. THE FLOWERS OF MANCHESTER"

Oh England's finest football team, its record truly great
Its proud successes mocked by a twist of fate
Eight met who'll never play again,
Who met destruction there
The Flowers of English football,
The Flowers of Manchester.

STRIKING SEASONS

The goals just keep on coming...

1. **46** Denis Law (1963/64)
2. **44** Ruud van Nistelrooy (2002/03)
3. **39** Denis Law (1964/65)
4. **36** Ruud van Nistelrooy (2001/02)
5. **34** Tommy Taylor (1956/57)
6. **33** Billy Whelan (1956/57)
   33 David Herd (1965/66)
8. **32** Dennis Viollet (1959/60)
   32 George Best (1967/68)
10. **31** Brian McClair (1987/88)
11. **30** Jack Rowley (1948/49)
    30 Jack Rowley (1951/52)
    30 Denis Law (1968/69)
    30 Ruud van Nistelrooy (2003/04)

TALLEST REDS

Despite the terrace song which exaggerated his height, Big Jim Holton was actually 6ft 1in – but these were the real giants

1. **6ft 5in Peter Fletche**r forward (1972/73)
   6ft 5in Peter Schmeichel goalkeeper (1991-99)
3. **6ft 4in Gary Pallister** defender (1989-1998)
   6ft 4in Gordon McQueen defender (1978-1985)
5. **6ft 3in Gary Walsh** goalkeeper (1986-1995)
   6ft 3in Harry Moger goalkeeper (1986-1995)
7. **6ft 2in Gary Bailey** goalkeeper (1978-1986)
   6ft 2in Paul McGrath defender (1982-1999)

6ft 2in Fred Goodwin defender (1954-1960)
6ft 2in Mark Bosnich goalkeeper (1989-1991 and 1999-2001)
6ft 2in Raimond Van Der Gouw goalkeeper (1996–2001)
6ft 2in Steve Patterson defender (1976-1980)

TARTAN REDS: 11 GREAT SCOTS

The two finest managers in United history (no, that doesn't include the Doc) came from north of the border, and the Reds have a distinguished history of Scottish players. Here's an uncompromising bunch

1. Jim Leighton
Born: Renfrewshire. It all went wrong in the 1990 Cup final, when he was dropped for the replay, but Jim recovered to play on elsewhere for another eight seasons.

2. Darren Fletcher
Born: Edinburgh. OK, so he's not a full–back, but he's in this XI ahead of the likes of Alex Forsyth as the sole contemporary upholder of the tradition at Old Trafford.

3. Arthur Albiston
Born: Edinburgh. Full-back of grace and style, whose lengthy career encompassed four different managers.

4. Pat Crerand
Born: Glasgow. Harder than granite and Redder than a very red thing, Crerand provided the steel that enabled Law, Best and Charlton to work their glory.

5. Gordon McQueen
Born: Kilbirnie. Lanky centre-back whose late goal in the 1979 FA Cup final set up a memorably mad last five minutes.

6. Martin Buchan
Born: Aberdeen. The half-back and captain remained cool through the botched and scraggy relegation days to emerge, his hair still immaculately groomed, to lift the FA Cup in 1977.

7. Willie Morgan
Born: Sauchie. The longest-serving United player never to win a medal: not a record to be proud of, perhaps, but a record nonetheless.

11. TARTAN REDS

Leighton

Fletcher Buchan McQueen Albiston

Crerand

Morgan Macari McClair

Jordan Law

Two of United's finest
managers also stemmed
from north of the border.

8. Lou Macari
Born: Edinburgh. Nippy midfielder whose fondness for a wager led him into big
trouble during a management career which took in Swindon Town, West Ham
United, Celtic and Stoke City.

9. Joe Jordan
Born: Lanark. Scary centre-forward, whose manual intervention in a crucial World
Cup qualifier against Wales in 1977 pre-dated Maradona by nearly a decade.

10. Brian McClair
Born: Airdrie. Striker who wanted to be a maths teacher, now holding up the
numbers as United's reserve-team boss.

11. Denis Law
Born: Aberdeen. The King. No more need be said about the fisherman's son.

Alex Ferguson and Matt Busby
Joint managers.

TEAMS WE LOVE TO HATE

Mourinho is going to have to go some way to make a mark on this table

1. Liverpool
The eternal rivals. It's about time they started playing their part. Actually, no it's not.

2. City
Deluded neighbours who don't win trophies.

3. Arsenal
More a football rivalry rather than one born out of mutual loathing. It's not like fans in the Highbury library wind us up, is it?

4. Leeds United
"We all hate Leeds scum." Reds sing it for a reason…

5. Bolton Wanderers
Belligerent, moustached, pie-eating yonners.

6. Chelsea
The plastic club for mercenaries and tourists. Chart climbers. Average crowds were 21,000 a decade ago. Home of the bungling Kenyon.

7. Aston Villa
Given the number of empty seats at Villa Park when United don't visit, a classic case of: 'You've only come to see United.'

8. Galatasaray
Old wounds run deep for their appalling treatment of United's players and fans in the mid-1990s.

9. Everton
The one-song-Scousers who work hard at being mediocre.

10. Newcastle
Overweight, incomprehensible fans who get married in their replica shirts and shout 'Toon' at their black-and-white dogs.

11. Sheffield Wednesday
Fallen average-sized club whose fans got lippy in the mid-1990s.

11 TERRACE HEROES

Sealey

G. Neville   May   Holton   Heinze

Stiles

Whiteside

Milne

Cantona

Hughes   Law

Ralph Milne? Like Howard the Duck, Ralph was a new breed of hero... cherished because he was an utterly useless kind of hero.

TERRACE HEROES

Not many would list this as their all-time greatest United side, but every player within it won the respect of hardcore fans

1. Les Sealey
Rescued the 1990 FA Cup final, played in the League Cup final with his knee in pieces and starred in the 1991 Cup Winners' Cup final only after visiting a faith healer to reduce the swelling in the joint. All the while making Bez look a model of sanity. Died all too young in 2001.

2. Gary Neville
The Scouser-phobic full-back has a special place in United hearts.

3. Gabriel Heinze
How travelling Reds love to wind up their England-supporting rivals by chanting "Argentina" every time he scythes in with a shin-threatening challenge. Which is about ten times a match.

4. David May
Once a European villain after he was horribly exposed against Gothenburg, May became a hero the moment he hijacked the celebrations after the Champions League final in 1999. A non-playing sub, there he is orchestrating the applause as schoolkids across the globe ask: "Dad, who's he?"

5. Jim Holton
"Six feet two, eyes of blue, big Jim Holton's after you," goes the favourite Stretford End chant. And he'd have caught you too, if he could have borrowed a motorbike.

6. Nobby Stiles
Blind as a bat, bald as a coot, couldn't run: how they loved Sir Matt's hard man. As Mrs Thatcher might have said: every team needs its Nobby.

7. Eric Cantona
Eight years after he retired, his name is still chanted more often than any contemporary player.

8. Norman Whiteside
If he had done nothing else in his United career, the game in April 1988 at Anfield – when he came off the bench and single-handedly terrorised a then rampant Liverpool to secure a 3–3 draw – would have cast him forever in United legend.

9. Mark Hughes
Hughsie's welcoming chant always sounded like the brand name of a machine gun. But then "Uzi" was a pretty appropriate thing to call the bull-like centre-forward.

10. Denis Law
While the main stand thermos-flask-carriers admired Charlton and the women loved Best, for the lads on the Stretford End, Law was the man.

> BLIND AS A BAT, BALD AS A COOT, COULDN'T RUN: HOW THEY LOVED NOBBY STILES, SIR MATT'S HARD MAN

11. Ralph Milne
Fergie's worst signing – so bad you had to laugh. But only after he had long left the club. It must have been the fans' innate sense of comedy that made them vote him into the top 100 favourite United players in 2000.

THINGS ERIC DOES AFTER HE RETIRES

We don't know why but we still love him...

1. Eric appears on a BBC documentary
In it, he says Alex Ferguson is the greatest manager in the history of the game.

2. Eric takes the role of Monsieur de Foix, the French ambassador
In Shekhar Kapur's movie *Elizabeth*, released in 1998. Also in the cast are hugely excited United fans Christopher Eccleston (who plays the Duke of Norfolk) and Angus Deayton (as Waad, the Chancellor of the Exchequer).

3. Eric features in a new beach football venture
This involves touring the sand spots of Europe throughout the summer of 2001: "I was born for this game," he says.

4. Eric brings his beach circus to London
Playing on a specially imported sand-pitch in Hyde Park. A crowd of loyal Reds – some of whom may well have taken alcohol – cheer his every move.

5. Eric nutmegs John Scales
Classy move during a France v England beach international.

6. Eric appears in the 2002 World Cup Nike ads
Eric is the master of a slave ship filled with the world's top footballers, who play for their freedom to an Elvis remix soundtrack.

7. Eric joins in the ovation for Real Madrid's Ronaldo
During the 2003 Champions League quarter-final at Old Trafford, in which the Brazilian takes United's defence apart with two superb goals.

8. Eric grows a beard
We're not just talking Le Stubble.

9. Eric takes the lead part in the French comedy L'Outremangeur
In this 2003 film ('The Over-eater'), the King wears a fat suit, though later off-screen sightings suggest this may not have been strictly necessary.

10. Eric turns up at Euro 2004 announcing he is supporting England
The French team, he says, is "full of prima donnas who need constantly to be told how good they are."

11. Eric used the mother-word in a live phone-in on MUTV
No viewer complains. And he still has a beard.

TOP APPEARANCES BY A PLAYER

Give that man a testimonial. The figures are to the end of the 2004/05 season, so Giggs. Keane and Gary Neville are still on the rise

1. **Sir Bobby Charlton** (1956-73) 754 games
2. **Bill Foulkes** (1952-69) 682
3. **Ryan Giggs** (1990-) 622
4. **Alex Stepney** (1966-78) 535
5. **Tony Dunne** (1960-73) 530
6. **Joe Spence** (1919-33) 510
7. **Arthur Albiston** (1974-88) 482
8. **Brian McClair** (1987-98) 471
9. **George Best** (1963-74) 470
10. **Roy Keane** (1993-) 461
11. **Bryan Robson** (1981-94) 460
    Gary Neville (1992-) 460

TWENTY-THREE MILLION CHINESE CAN'T BE WRONG

Reds are here, Reds are there... a MORI poll conducted by the club suggested United boast a total worldwide fanbase of around 75 million, with the following geographical hot-spots.

1. **China** 23.6 million
2. **UK** 9.7 million
3. **South Africa** 5.9 million
4. **Malaysia** 3.5 million
5. **USA** 3.2 million
6. **Australia** 3.2 million
7. **Thailand** 3.2 million
8. **Japan** 2.3 million
9. **Poland** 2.2 million
10. **Singapore** 2.1 million
11. **Canada** 1.4 million

UNITED BY NICKNAME

11 other Red Devils

1. The Red Devils
The most famous other Red Devils are the British Army's parachute regiment and free-fall display team. Based in Wiltshire, they are in constant demand to chuck themselves out of planes.

2. Bryant's Red Devils
This is the only establishment in north Georgia (the US state, not the former Soviet satellite) to buy a red nose American pit bull terrier. "We strive to produce quality, healthy, even-tempered dogs with the ability to do it all!" boast Bryant's.

3. Red Devils Merano
These Red Devils don't get penalised for handling the ball. It's actually the point of the game. They are a professional handball side in northern Italy.

4. Red Devil Cheerleaders
This troop of women including such pom-pom legends as Babett, Judith, Nancy and Saskia, are available for hire all across Germany.

5. Gunnedah Red Devils
Founded in a rural part of New South Wales in 1883, these Red Devils are one of Australia's oldest rugby clubs.

6. Woodquarter Red Devils
Did you know that baseball is actually quite popular in Austria? Well, it is, and these Red Devils play in the Landesliga Ost.

7. Mexico City Red Devils

What is it with baseball and this nickname? Here is another team who call themselves the Red Devils, although it sounds better in Spanish – *Diablo Rojos*.

8. C.B. Murcia

This junior basketball side in Spain are known as the Red Devils. Strangely, their web site shows three of their players showing their underpants.

9. Belgium

The nickname of the Belgian national football team is also the Red Devils, which upset a group of church groups in South Korea before the World Cup finals were staged there in 2002.

10. The Red Devils

A support network and charity based in Maryland for families living with breast cancer. Their name was inspired by Katherine Russell Rich's book *The Red Devil, To Hell With Cancer And Back*.

11. Dickinson College Red Devils

The various sports teams of this American college in Carlisle, Pennsylvania – which include their brand of football, basketball, volleyball, lacrosse, and yes, soccer – are also known as the Red Devils. Other sporting young US collegiate Red Devils can be found at Eureka College, Illinois and at Springville high school in Utah, where the school board recently rejected a request by some residents that the longtime Red Devil mascot be changed. According to the local newspaper, the mascot was based on the logo of the Red Devil Cement Co. which laid the foundation when the school was built, and is seen by traditionalists as "a symbol of power and strength" and by others, many of them newcomers, as offensive." We know which side we're on.

> THE DICKINSON COLLEGE RED DEVILS MONIKER DOESN'T JUST APPLY TO THEIR SOCCER TEAM

UNITED SONGS

Some suggestions for your Desert Island Discs playlist

1. Manchester United Number One (A Fans Anthem)

Richie Dew's painful ballad didn't trouble the charts. Why? Take a listen to the lyrics and all becomes clear. "Beckham, Scholes and Giggs and Cole. And Charlton and the rest. And we love you Uncle Georgie, you're the Best."

2. Belfast Boy
Don Fardon's homage to George Best reached number 32 in 1970.

3. Glory! Glory! Man United
Recorded for the 1983 FA Cup Final, Ron Atkinson and his team managed to get all the way to number 13 in the charts.

4. You're In My Heart
"You're Celtic, United, but baby I've decided you're the best team I've ever seen" sang Rod Stewart in his 1977 hit. Not the best chat-up line, is it?

5. Manchester United
United were clearly not inspired by their 1976 FA Cup final song as they lost 1-0 to Southampton. The record itself limped to number 50 in the charts.

6. Come On You Reds
In May 1994 United brought denim-clad rockers Status Quo on board to rework their hit *Burning Bridges*. This helped United become the first club to reach number one.

7. We're Gonna Do It Again
Clearly ahead of the times, United enlisted Britain's early answer to Eminem, a white Mancunian rapper called Stryker, to rhyme on their 1995 FA Cup final song. Stryker hasn't been heard of since.

8. United (We Love You)
But the British public decided they didn't love this song, recorded to celebrate winning the Premier League in 1993. It spent just two weeks in the chart.

9. Move Move Move (The Red Tribe)
Dreadful title. Dreadful song. Criminally released not once, but twice in 1996, and reached number 6 in the charts. The culprits? The United FA Cup squad of 1997.

10. Lift It High (All About Belief)
On the brink of the Treble, the 1999 Manchester United squad sang along to this pseudo-Oasis effort.

11. Outstanding
Who persuaded Andy Cole to record this appalling record? Cole doesn't sing, he raps, and very badly over the Gap Band's classic.

Reds partial to this sort of thing might care to note that Cherry Red have released *Come On You Reds*, a CD of 20 'classic' tunes in homage to Manchester United for a tenner, including some older – and perhaps understandably – rarer tunes.

USA, SWAZILAND... 11 DODGY FRIENDLY LOCATIONS

You're having a laugh, Boss

1. The United States, 1950
United's players sailed to New York on the Queen Mary for a mammoth post-season tour. However, the glamour faded soon after the team docked in Manhattan. Results were poor and the travelling, mostly by train, wore the team out. Expenses of $5 a day went entirely on meals, denying the players an opportunity to spend in this consumers' paradise. The night before the team were due to sail back to Southampton, winger Charlie Mitten received a call in United's Times Square hotel. It was an offer of unbelievable money to play in Colombia. The news caused a sensation. Mitten never took the boat, opting for a flight to Bogota via Miami instead. He got his money but he never played for United again.

2. Swaziland, 1983
United's players had barely finished celebrating the 1983 FA Cup win before they flew to Africa for a post-season tour. United played Tottenham Hotspur twice in the Lobamba national stadium, winning one and losing one. In between, United and Spurs combined to form a single team: TottMan. This bizarre amalgamation beat a Swaziland XI 6–1.

3. Singapore, 2001
Two days after Ruud van Nistelrooy and Juan Sebastian Veron made their United debuts in Kuala Lumpur, Malaysia, United unveiled a third international outfield player – left-winger Fabien Barthez. The 50,000 Singaporean United fans who filled the national stadium cheered Barthez's every touch – hardly surprising given that they had even roared their approval when the names of the match sponsors had been announced.

4. Tehran, 1975
Inconceivable now, but in 1975 United travelled to (pre-revolution) Iran to commence a global summer tour. From there, the Reds pushed east to Bangkok (where manager Tommy Docherty made an untimely appearance – he was sent off), Hong Kong, Jakarta, Perth, Sydney, Melbourne, Auckland and Los Angeles.

5. South Africa, 1993

United played against Arsenal at Ellis Park, Johannesburg, and the Kaiser Chiefs at the FNB Stadium, Soweto. The difference between the crowds at the two games was stark – a predominantly white crowd at Ellis Park contrasting with an almost all-black turnout at the later game.

6. Australia, 1999

One for the anoraks this, but in 1999 United played four consecutive games in stadiums which held 80,000, 98,000, 95,000 and 110,000. The first, at Wembley, sealed the Double. The second, in Barcelona, the Treble. The third, at the giant Melbourne Cricket Ground, staged United's first game since the Treble. Then, in Sydney in the newly built Olympic Stadium, almost 80,000 Aussie fans paid between £35 and £70 to see the Socceroos beaten 1–0 in a physical and unfulfilling game.

7. Bermuda, 1987

The 1987 mid-season tour of Bermuda is one the club would rather forget. United may have won both games 4-1 and sourced a callow Shaun Goater, but rookie goalkeeper Gary Walsh was kicked violently in the head, sustaining an injury from which he took years to recover. As well as his players, Ferguson had himself to worry about, as he and assistant Archie Knox made appearances in United's injury-hit side. The injuries were so bad that in one game a British ex-pat came on as substitute.

8. Molde, 1991

Tiny Norwegian club Molde FK were managed by ex-Man City player and current Norway coach Åge Hareide when United, with new keeper Peter Schmeichel, won 3-1 in front of 3,500. Molde's significance became apparent four years later when striker Ole Gunnar Solskjaer swapped life by a fjord for one by the ship canal. The transfer cash helped Molde played Champions League football in 1999/2000.

9. Shanghai, 1999

When West Brom visited China in the 1970s, their players had the chance to visit the Great Wall. The card-school-loving Black Country sophisticates coined the line: "Seen one wall, seen 'em all." When United visited China for the first time in 1999 they did see a wall – that of hundreds of police protecting them from fans outside the Shanghai stadium which was full to its 80,000 capacity. United beat China's top side Shenua with class finishes from Teddy Sheringham and Ole Gunnar Solskjaer.

10. Bornholm Island, 1987

United have often gone to Scandinavia pre-season, but the remote Swedish island of Bornholm was an odd choice. Travel options were limited and most of the players were seasick on the ferry. Still, they beat Danish side B1903 Copenhagen 3-2 in front of 2,500 fans – in a field with a rope around it.

11. Tokyo, 2005
That's what United planned for the summer of 2005, a friendly in the world's biggest city following on from games in Beijing, Hong Kong and Yokohama.

WARS OF THE ROSES

11 notable encounters with Leeds (you do remember Leeds, don't you?)

1. Handbags at Hillsborough 27 March 1965
Ill feeling prevailed when United's dexterous young Irish winger Johnny Giles fell out with Matt Busby and moved to Elland Road in 1963. In 1965, United reached their fourth consecutive FA Cup semi-final where they met, yes, Leeds. Both clubs were battling for success in league and Cup. In front of 65,000 at Hillsborough, Jack Charlton and Denis Law wrestled like schoolboys as players swapped punches. The game finished 0-0, with ref, managers and players all criticised for their conduct.

2. Battle stations on the Trent 31 March 1965
The replay was in Nottingham four days later where players fought again. Rival fans followed, with one running on the pitch and knocking the referee to the ground, and there were disturbances on the terraces with stories of fans being thrown into the River Trent confirmed by police. Leeds won the tie 1-0 with a last-minute Billy Bremner goal set up by, yes, Johnny Giles. Still, United finished the season as champions for the first time in eight years – on goal difference from Leeds.

> LEEDS HAD THE BEST OF THE ENCOUNTERS IN THE EARLY 1970S HAMMERING UNITED 5-1 IN 1972

3. Back to Hillsborough… 14 March 1970
Busby's third side peaked with 1968 European Cup

success. Leeds, meanwhile, consistently won major honours. In 1970, an ageing United team drew Leeds in the FA Cup semi-final. "The game was spoiled by the weather," recalls Johnny Giles of the 0-0 draw at Hillsborough.

4. ...and on to Villa Park... 23 March 1970

"The second game at Villa Park was in the top three that I ever played in," adds Giles. "There were no goals, but there was passion, great players and skill. It had everything except goals."

> HILLSBOROUGH LOOKED LIKE AN EGG WITH A WHOLE BOTTLE OF KETCHUP POURED OVER IT

5. ...and finally Burnden Park 26 March 1970

An impressive 173,500 people had watched the teams do battle by the time Leeds won the third game at Burnden Park, 1-0. "All the players were tired after three games in less than a week," concludes Giles.

6. A different league 11 October 1975

Leeds undoubtedly had the best of the early 1970s encounters, hammering United 5-1 at Elland Road in 1972. Then the Reds were relegated, to be greeted on their return to Leeds in 1975 with the song: "Where were you in '74?" Playing great football to capacity crowds, actually... Oh, and we won this one 2-1 too.

7. Once more to Hillsborough 23 April 1977

For the 1977 FA Cup semi-final at Hillsborough, both teams were allocated 21,000 tickets with Sheffield Wednesday receiving the 'neutral' 13,000. After United's allocation sold out, Mancunian touts bought up many of these tickets, and with Leeds not selling their allocation, one newspaper described the scene: "Within 15 minutes Manchester United were two-up, delighting a crowd which the Red of Lancashire so dominated the yellow and white of Yorkshire that Hillsborough looked like an egg with a whole bottle of tomato ketchup poured over it." United won 2-1 and went on to lift the Cup.

8. The McQueen/Jordan heist 23 August 1978

Leeds fans were stunned in 1978 when over a three-week period they lost their best two players, Gordon McQueen and Joe Jordan, for record fees... to Manchester United. When the following season the pair faced their old club wearing Red shirts, the insults flew. Seven minutes into the game United were awarded a corner at the Gelderd End and as McQueen moved forward the abuse got louder and by the time he reached the penalty area missiles were being thrown. His subsequent headed goal stunned the home fans.

9. Eric was on the wrong team 1991/92
Leeds were relegated in 1982 but returned to the top-flight under Howard Wilkinson in 1990. In a 17-day period over December 1991 and January 1992, they played United three times at Elland Road – first in the league, then in the League Cup and finally in the FA Cup. United won both the Cup ties and drew the league game, but Red smugness evaporated months later when Leeds, free to concentrate on the league, held their nerve and pipped United to the title. In the following public celebrations, Eric Cantona told the Yorkshire fans: "I don't know why. But I love you." We'll forget about that.

> LEEDS HAD LOST JUST ONE OF THEIR FIRST 14 LEAGUE GAMES. UNITED WON 3-2, WHICH MADE IT TWO

10. Knocking O'Leary off his perch 29 November 1998
In 1998, United returned from a gruelling 3-3 game in Barcelona to face a talented young Leeds side, managed by David O'Leary, who had lost just one of their first 14 league games. United won 3-2, which made it two…

11. We won the league at Elland Road 20 February 2000
Leeds topped the table when United visited Elland Road in February 2000. Andy Cole's superb solo goal brought United a 1-0 victory and provided the impetus for a sixth championship in eight years. Within weeks, United fans were noting the significance of the victory by singing: "We won the league at Elland Road."

WELSH REDS

Get your daffs out for the Taffs...

1. Tom Jones
Born: Penycae, nr Wrexham
The green, green grass of Old Trafford was home for 13 years in the 1920s and 1930s. That he only played 189 games suggested he was his era's Ronnie Johnsen.

2. Clayton Blackmore
Born: Neath
Utility player who, in the time when meaningful shirt numbers were handed out on the day, achieved the record of wearing every number from 2 to 14.

3. David Jones
Born: Ynysddu, near Monmouth

Not the most distinguished Welshman in United history, this Jones only played once in the first team, in December 1937. And they lost, 4-0 at Bradford Park Avenue.

4. Alan Davies
Born: Manchester

Davies's parents were Welsh, and immeasurably proud after he won international recognition soon after playing in the 1983 FA Cup final as a late replacement for Steve Coppell. But he was blighted by injury, and tragically killed himself in 1992 after clinical depression took hold.

5. Caesar Augustus Llewellyn Jenkins
Born: Builth

Newton Heath's bruiser of a captain (he weighed over 14 stone and stood only 5ft 10in) is noteworthy not only for his magnificent name, but also for the fact that, on retirement, he went on to be an inspector in the Birmingham constabulary.

6. Billy Meredith
Born: Chirk

The superstar of his era, the trickiest chancer in town, Meredith was rescued from City before going on to play over 300 times for the Reds. And this despite once leading a players' strike.

7. William Jackson
Born: Flint

Lively winger for Newton Heath, who was described in a contemporary newspaper report as "a hard worker, not blessed with any great science, who fails to supply us with what we need most – a few goals". It's a fair bet that his mum didn't put that cutting in her scrapbook.

> HE WEIGHED 14 STONE, STOOD 5FT 10IN AND WENT ON TO BECOME A POLICE INSPECTOR

8. Ron Davies
Born: Holywell

The original Big Ron scored four at Old Trafford once in 1969, but that was for Southampton. When the Doc bought him five years later he failed to score at all in ten appearances, all as sub.

9. Wyn Davies
Born: Caernarvon
The Mighty Wyn was a Frank O'Farrell panic buy from City in 1972. After four goals in 15 games, the Welsh speaker was moved on by the Doc. Subsequent clubs included Blackpool, Stockport County, Crewe Alexandra, Bangor City... oh and of course Arcadia Shepherds of South Africa.

10. Mark Hughes
Born: Wrexham
The incomparable Sparky was bought back from Barcelona in 1988 by Fergie for his second spell at the club that discovered him. One of the most popular players ever, his name rings out at Old Trafford whenever he returns.

11. Ryan Giggs
Born: Cardiff
He may talk deepest Salford but Giggs's heart lies in Wales. Besides, he says, his mum would never have spoken to him again had he opted to play for England, as he could have done after qualifying on residency grounds.

Mark Hughes: Player-manager

THE WISDOM OF GARY NEVILLE

The thoughts of Red Nev

1. "I still remember first coming across him in the youth teams. All of us local lads, such as Nicky Butt, me and Paul Scholes, wondered who this flash Cockney lad was."
On his best mate David Beckham, 2003

2. "What happened at the end was the biggest kick up the backside we could possibly have wished for. The whole evening was tough but to walk around at the end, it felt as low as it could get in your own stadium."
On having to parade around an emptying Old Trafford after being beaten by the new champions Chelsea, 2005

3. "To me, Chelsea could move their stadium to the middle of Harrods and win 15 championships on the trot, and even if you moved Old Trafford to downtown Beirut, they still wouldn't be as big as us."
Clearly not a big fan of Chelsea, 1998

4. "There definitely were thoughts in my head that (the game) would not go ahead. It was such an injustice, they could have done it to any of us next time."
On the England squad's threat to strike in protest at Rio Ferdinand being dropped for missing a drugs test, 2003

5. "We don't have a big problem with racism in this country, you can think of probably one or two incidents in the last five or ten years… The FA and the England team have always campaigned against racism very well. We have just got to be aware that it is not cheapened slightly by companies like Nike getting a lot of PR out of it for nothing." **On Nike's anti-racism campaign, 2005**

6. "I want United to be the greatest club in the world…and I firmly believe that Sky's ownership of the club will help United achieve that. If they don't buy us, they would buy another club, so we should be grateful they've chosen us."
Voice of the fans? Neville surprisingly backs Rupert Murdoch's bid in 1998

7. "We probably did have fights when we were really young. Not fights, but I threw a gun at you once and cut your eye."
Reminiscing about childhood japes with younger brother Phil, who claimed to have forgotten the brutal incident, 2002

> WE DIDN'T HAVE FIGHTS, BUT I THREW A GUN AT YOU ONCE

8. "It's always toilets…You'll be there in the loo and someone will come up and say: 'Good game the other day.'"
Neville's response when asked if a lot of people ask him about football, 2003

9. "I think it's because I nailed my colours to the mast pretty quickly. It's caused me quite a few problems in my relationship with opposition fans, but it's obviously endeared me to the United fans."
On why he's loved by United fans, 2003

10. "I constantly got on the teachers' nerves. I wanted to wear what I wanted to wear and couldn't see why I couldn't and got in ridiculous amounts of trouble for it…I was a pain in the backside." **The teenage fashion rebel, 2002**

11. "It will be a difficult couple of days. It's difficult now and it will be difficult tomorrow." **This was clearly a difficult phase for Neville**

WORK PERMITS REQUIRED

Reds from some way outside of Greater Manchester

1. Dwight Yorke
The smiley Tobagan scored in the bars of Manchester as often as he did on the pitch.

2. Gabriel Heinze
Heinze's somewhat dodgy lineage stretches back to Germans who settled in Argentina immediately after World War 2. But at least his mum's Italian.

3. Eric Djemba Djemba
Cameroon's hard man, bought to fill Roy Keane's boots. Alas, his feet were way too small.

> HE WAS BOUGHT TO FILL ROY KEANE'S BOOTS. ALAS. HIS FEET WERE WAY TOO SMALL

4. Quinton Fortune
Once the most sought after young player in Africa.

5. Tim Howard
One of three Yanks on United's books simultaneously. Wouldn't put your mortgage on him when any team managed by José Mourinho has a free kick in the last minute of a cup tie at Old Trafford, however.

6. Jonathan Spector
He is a young American.

7. Juan Sebastian Veron
Argentina's finest was, as Churchill said of the Soviet Union, an enigma wrapped in a mystery.

8. Diego Forlan
He came from Uruguay and made the Scousers cry.

9. Kleberson
Brazilian World Cup winner. Apparently.

10. Floribert Ngalula
Young Senegalese striker learning his trade in the Academy.

11. Kenny Cooper
Baltimore-born centre-forward, had a time on loan at Oldham.

X-FILES

11 out there Red facts

1. John Sutcliffe

United's goalkeeper in 1903/04, Sutcliffe was the last person to play at international level for England in both football and rugby union.

2. The boycott

In October 1930, 3,000 United fans turned up at Hulme Town Hall to protest at the club's form. United were bottom of the league having not picked up a point in their first ten games of the season. Fans decided to boycott the game against Arsenal the following day and just 23,406 showed – well down on the 50,000 that would usually attend the fixture. United lost.

3. Is-ra-el...

The first non-European team to visit Old Trafford were Hapoel Tel Aviv for a friendly in September 1951. United beat the Israelis 6-0 in a game watched by just 12,000. Red Star Belgrade had been the first foreign team to visit Old Trafford, four months earlier, as part of the Festival of Britain.

4. Shoot now!

The 1952 Charity Shield between United and Newcastle was shown live on BBC television, yet they only covered 50 minutes of the game. Luckily for the cameras, they caught five of the game's six goals as the Geordies were vanquished 4–2.

5. Lighting-up time

In 1958, Salford rugby league club hired Old Trafford to experiment playing a game under floodlights. Over 8,000 watched them beat Leeds. Salford used the Red Devils nickname before United.

6. Real friends

Real Madrid were generous to United after the Munich air disaster, playing a series of friendly games. In October 1960, Madrid – who had won the first four European Cups – destroyed United 6-1 at Old Trafford. In the return game the following month United got a bit closer: 6-5.

7. The goalie who scored

In December 1973, United's top scorer was goalkeeper Alex Stepney – with two goals. Stepney scored penalties against Birmingham and Leicester, but missed from the spot in the home defeat to Wolverhampton Wanderers. He'd also scored in a pre-season friendly shoot-out against Uruguayan side Penarol. In 1972/73, Bobby Charlton was United's top league scorer with six goals, a miserable feat which wasn't matched until Sammy McIlroy finished top of the United goalscoring charts with six strikes in... 1973/74.

8. Hoop dreams

In 1985, United considered building a 9,000-seat indoor arena on the number one car park opposite Old Trafford to house the Manchester United basketball team. Martin Edwards had visions of a Barça style sports club. Sadly, he didn't have the money to fund it and the car park remained in use on a Sunday as a market.

9. A pub for promotion

United half-back Frank Barson was promised his own pub if he captained the club back to the First Division in 1925. He did just that and was promptly rewarded with the keys to a hotel in Ardwick Green. On opening night, a host of admirers packed into the hotel, but Barson was soon so fed up with the fawning and flattery that, after 15 minutes, he chucked the keys to the head waiter and left, telegraphing his wife to cancel delivery of the furniture.

10. Norman alone

Just 7,000 Reds showed for the 1992 testimonial of 1980s terrace hero Norman Whiteside. Unfortunately for the Ulsterman, the game came a week after United had blown the league title and fans were not in charitable mood. It was the last-ever game that fans stood on the Stretford End.

11. Kids' stuff

A record 61,599 watched the two FA Youth Cup final games between holders United and Leeds in 1993: 30,562 watched the first leg at Old Trafford, 31,037 seeing the second. Leeds won the competition.

YEAH, IT'S HIM

11 celebrity fans who actually turn out to matches

1. Christopher Eccleston
Dr Who himself sets the Tardis down in the North Stand most home games.

2. Angus Deayton
Coke-snorting fan of hookers – and there's no allegedly about it.

3. Richard Wilson
He doesn't believe it when United lose.

4. Eamonn Holmes
Used to be up with the lark every day, talking blarney.

5. Terry Christian
Professional Mancunian and Red author.

6. Tony Wilson
Broadcaster, Factory man and undisputed heavyweight champion of professional Mancunians.

7. Bez
The Happy Mondays freaky dancer and *Celebrity Big Brother* winner likes to shake his maracas in the Stretford End.

8. Debbie Horsfield
The top-notch television writer, responsible for *Cutting It*, can be spotted with her sisters at many a European away game.

9. John Squire
Once of Manchester's finest, the Stone Roses. Still bangs the drum for the Reds.

10. Mani
Squire's old colleague and *Soccer AM* regular, now playing bass in Primal Scream.

11. Terry Hall
The former Specials man has kept the Red faith for three decades.

YOU WIN NOTHING WITH KIDS: 11 RED PRODIGIES

The youngest players in United history – dates are their first-team debuts

1. David Gaskell, goalkeeper
24 October 1956 v Manchester City (Charity Shield); aged 16 years 19 days.

2. Jeff Whitefoot, full-back
15 April 1950 v Portsmouth (league); 16 years 105 days.

3. Ian Moir, forward
5 April 1960 v Shamrock Rovers (friendly); 16 years 172 days.

4. Sammy McIlroy, midfield
21 January 1971 v Bohemians (friendly); 16 years 172 days.

5. Duncan Edwards, half-back
4 April 1953 v Cardiff City (league); 16 years 185 days.

6. Roy Morton, full-back
18 May 1972 v Real Mallorca (friendly); 16 years 202 days.

7. Willie Anderson, winger
28 December 1963 v Burnley (league); 16 years 338 days.

8. Norman Whiteside, midfield
24 April 1982 v Brighton (league); 16 years 352 days.

DR WHO SETS THE TARDIS DOWN IN THE NORTH STAND FOR MOST HOME GAMES

9. Alex Dawson, forward
22 April 1957 v Burnley (league); 17 years 60 days; scored.

10. Peter Coyne, forward
24 April 1976 v Leicester City (league); 17 years 162 days; scored.

11. Jimmy Nicholson, half-back,
24 August 1960 v Everton (league); 17 years 177 days.

ZANY JOBS OUT OF FOOTBALL

It's all in my spare time, Boss

1. Steve Bruce, crime writer

Steve Bruce, the manager and former United centre-back, is the author of three novels of pulp fiction (*Striker!*, *Defender!* and *Sweeper!*) narrated by a crime-solving football coach called Steve Barnes, who used to play centre-back for Mulcaster United. Bruce started writing after leaving Huddersfield in 2000, but stopped when he became Birmingham boss. These days his main writing action concerns owner David Sullivan's cheques.

2. John Fitchett, actor/theatre manager

Fitchett squeezed in just 18 appearances and one goal for United in his two spells at the club. He found more success as an actor in Edwardian impresario Fred Karno's theatrical company. Karno's was famed for giving debuts to Stan Laurel and Charlie Chaplin. Fitchett, though, didn't get the Hollywood breaks of his predecessors and, after Karno went bust, was last heard of running a cinema in Plymouth in 1934.

3. Charlie Mitten, sword dancer

> HIS HARMONICA PLAYING WAS NOT THE END OF MITTEN'S TALENTS

His renowned harmonica playing was not the end of Mitten's talents. Brought up in Scotland, he danced around claymores in his youth and insisted reels and larks helped his footballing skills. "I could get into my stride quicker, turn in those tight spaces – you're twirling and twisting and you've still got your balance," he said. When he managed Newcastle (from 1958 to 1961) he tried to introduce his players to sword dancing. That Magpies line-up included George Eastham and Ivor Allchurch but they danced, Mitten noted sadly, "like bloody shire horses".

4. Arnie Sidebottom, Test cricketer

The statistics aren't that glorious. Played: 1; batting average: 1; wickets taken: 1; runs per wicket: 65. But Arnie Sidebottom can still claim to be the only Manchester United footballer to have played in a Test match against Australia – winning his cap in England's last Ashes-winning team. A fringe centre-back in Doc's Red Army, Sidebottom played 20 times for United in the mid-1970s. By 1985, he was turning out for Huddersfield in the winter and Yorkshire in the summer, when he got a surprise call into the England side. His son Ryan got a solitary test cap, too, in 2001.

5. Thomas Wilcox, world punchball champion

Punchball, essentially baseball for those who reckon bats are for wimps, was very popular on American street corners in the late 19th century. Wilcox had emigrated to America in 1879 and became so adept at the game he won the world championship (though as with many American sports the term 'world' was somewhat exaggerated). Returning to England after the professional punchball circuit failed to take off, Wilcox took up goalkeeping and made two appearances for United in 1908/09. After surviving four years active service in World War 1, he opened a tobacconists shop in Blackpool, where he died in 1962.

6. Mickey Thomas, freelance printer

It was, you understand, entirely an act of loyalty to the crown that led the Welsh dynamo to pass lots of pictures of Her Majesty the Queen on small rectangles of paper round the Wrexham dressing-room in the summer of 1993. And it was just his enthusiasm for the artistic merit of the project that encouraged him to give 80 of the said items to some of the club's trainees. The police were less impressed and a circuit judge, for some reason, thought he was trying to pass off counterfeit tenners and jailed him for 18 months.

7. Charlie Moore, busker

A full-back who made 328 appearances in the 1920s, Moore was a keen drinking buddy of team-mate Joe Spence. Once, after celebrating a win in Portsmouth, the pair continued their pub carousing out on to the pavement. They popped down a hat and managed to accrue the sum total of 11d – 3d of which was said to come from a passing United director who felt rather sorry for the pair.

8. Phil Neville, England cricket captain

The younger Neville was a batsman at Lancashire, where he was on the books as a junior, reckoned good enough to make it to Test level. The international selectors thought so too and he was made captain of the England under-16 side which included Andrew Flintoff and Steve Harmison. Thus, when he was tossed the arm band during a flurry of substitutions in an England football international in 2003, he became the only United player to captain his country at representative level at both cricket and football.

9. Ian Ure, prison social worker
Since retiring from football in 1976, former United defender Ure has worked as a prison social worker in some of Scotland's toughest prisons like Glasgow's Barlinnie. "The prisoners often weigh me up," said Ure. "Some of them can't believe that I once played football. They used to try and wind me up and say that I was a shite player. Nowadays, most of them can't remember me. Once, I came up against someone who I'd played against. He was doing life for murder. He couldn't believe that I was working in a prison because he thought that I would have made a fortune from playing. Except I just missed out on the big money. I bump into my lads on the outside all the time. You know it's a lad from the inside because they call me Mr Ure."

10. Steve Coppell, gent and a scholar
When he wasn't surging down the wing for United in the 1970s, Scouser Coppell was a full-time economics student at Liverpool University. "I told Tommy Docherty that I had an option to delay my studies," recalls Coppell of signing for United, "but he said, 'absolutely no chance, football can be finished at the click of your finger, academic qualifications are with you for life'." With that, Coppell lived and studied in Liverpool, training alone, except for a weekly Tuesday night session at the Cliff.

> IT'S UNLIKELY ANY OTHER RED CAN SAY HE PLAYED IN ANFIELD FOR ECONOMICS DURING THE WEEK

"It would never happen now, and it would only be with a character like Doc that that happened then," said Coppell. "If United didn't have a mid-week game I'd play in goal in the university interdepartmental league. We got to the cup final, losing 6-1 to geography, not one of my better games!" It's unlikely that any other Red can say that he played for United at Anfield at the weekend – and in Anfield for economics during the week.

11. John Gidman, businessman
When the former United right-back's football career ended in the late 1980s, the Militant MP Derek Hatton asked Gidman what he was up to. "I told him that I was thinking of building a golf range," said Gidman. "He offered help in getting land and I bought 26 acres for £10,000 freehold in a good area of Liverpool. I didn't know that the police were onto him and that Neil Kinnock wanted him out of the Labour party.

11. THE ALL TIME GREATEST RED 11

Schmeichel

Byrne Pallister Ferdinand Irwin

Robson Keane Edwards

Charlton Cantona Best

Argue with this one. We did for half the night. Can you really leave out the King, in favour of the God? Just how good was Busby Babes captain Roger Byrne? And could any team survive against a midfield of Robson, Keane and Edwards? We did contemplate a sub's bench – but that opened up another half a night's debate, so we'll leave it at this.

And I didn't know that my phone was being bugged. Kenny Dalglish agreed to open the golf range but the day it was due to open, and with all cameras there, Kenny pulled out and said that he would get the sack if he opened it. I gave a false story to reporters that he was buying John Barnes and got the snooker player John Parrott to open it instead. I later found out Kenny's chairman knew what was going on with Hatton. After six months, eight heavies arrested me for fraud. They tried to charge me but it didn't reach court, and I wasn't found guilty of anything."

"The Luther Blissetts don't exist. Only Luther Blissett exists"

Italian anarchists, who used the AC Milan striker's identity in court, 'clarify' matters

If this Rough Guide has struck a chord, do yourself a favour and seek out the Rough Guide to Cult Football, probably the oddest football book ever written, covering iconic stars, pointless clubs, the cups that time forgot and Pelé's secret career as a guitar axe-man. Failing that, you may enjoy the Rough Guides to Superheroes, Cult Movies, Cult Fiction and Muhammad Ali. Essential, compact reading, these books are almost as good as having three points in the bag.